Reel Chance Fish Tales

Reel Chance
Fish Tales

Captain Rick Percy

Xulon Press

Xulon Press
2301 Lucien Way #415
Maitland, FL 32751
407.339.4217
www.xulonpress.com

© 2017 by Captain Rick Percy

All rights reserved solely by the author. The author guarantees all contents are original and do not infringe upon the legal rights of any other person or work. No part of this book may be reproduced in any form without the permission of the author. The views expressed in this book are not necessarily those of the publisher.

Edited by Xulon Press.

Printed in the United States of America.

ISBN-13: 9781545620724

Dedication

For Dad

If he were here today, and I handed him this book, his exact words would have been: "Well who'd have thunk it"?

Acknowledgments

A special thanks to Dean Ray for inspiring me to write this book, to Mac and Pierre McGowan for helping with the title and editing, and to Donna Miseyko, Dawn Shepard, and Miles Murdaugh for their assistance in proofreading and making necessary changes.

Contents

Foreword...xiii
Introduction..xvii

Chapter 1 The Early Years 1
Chapter 2 Boats...7
Chapter 3 Mama 26
Chapter 4 A Pig..30
Chapter 5 Henry 32
Chapter 6 Storms 35
Chapter 7 Kersplash!...................................41
Chapter 8 Dolphin......................................45
Chapter 9 The Emory Professor 52
Chapter 10 From a Zero to a Hero 55
Chapter 11 Brays Island Tournament 60
Chapter 12 My First, and Last, King Mackerel Charter ..66
Chapter 13 One Hook, Three Fish 72
Chapter 14 Big Trout 75
Chapter 15 Jaws 79
Chapter 16 The Law 82
Chapter 17 Oops!.......................................86
Chapter 18 Divine Intervention 89
Chapter 19 Baits 92
Chapter 20 Tackle 99

Conclusion 103

Foreword

Several years ago, I received a frantic call. "Jim! I need your help . . . again!"

"What's wrong, Rick? You okay?"

"No," he answered, voice wavering. "I did a dumb thing. I pulled the Lake & Bay out at the landing and drove her all the way home with the 250 running!"

"Did you shut her off?" I asked.

"Yes," he answered.

"Well, check the oil. If it looks okay, hook the hose up and see if she'll crank. Remember, it's a four-stroke and a Yamaha to boot. Likely, the only damage might be the water pump impeller."

After a little coaxing, he cranked the 250 and she ran perfectly. Only thing he could say was, "Darn thing's too quiet!

That was not my first encounter with Captain Rick Percy. In midsummer 2009, I answered my cell phone, and the voice at the other end, somewhat strained, asked, "Mr. Goller?" I acknowledged and the voice went on, "I need your help." The voice introduced himself as Rick Percy, a local Beaufort fishing guide. He stated he had livewell pump issues on his Pathfinder 22, a charter the next day, and that I'd been recommended as a marine electrical tech.

I agreed to come over the next morning. After introductory handshakes, Rick said, "I guess I should ask how much you charge."

"Seventy-five an hour," I replied. "A hundred and twenty-five an hour if you help."

"That's fair," he stated with a chuckle. "I won't be helping."

As I worked, we chatted, swapped fishing stories (and lies), and before that first repair job was finished, we'd become fast friends.

The bond formed that day has lasted these past eight years through many of Rick's boat repair issues, fishing trips full of success along with the inevitable fair share of mishaps, countless commiserations centered on what we "shoulda/coulda done," and our pledge to each other to get it right the "next time." Through it all, the love of fishing and boating has bound our lives together in true friendship.

Captain Rick Percy is a quiet, soft-spoken man who never boasts about his angling skills. When I probe him about the day's success, he'll simply state, "We did okay," then proceed to tell me "okay" means twenty-plus redfish, a dozen sea trout, several flounder, and a handful of jacks, blues, ladyfish, and sharks. "Oh . . . and we did get a forty-pound cobia sight-fishing the Broad River to round out the day." *Quietly understated* sums up Captain Rick.

Rick is not only a skilled angler, but also a true conservationist who cares about his catch more than the money he makes catching.

FOREWORD

Spend five minutes with him, and his genuine concern for the future of his sport becomes crystal-clear. He will take every precaution to ensure the future of angling for us, our children, and our grandchildren, not just for himself.

As I read through his manuscript, I imagined Rick Percy was simply talking to me through his writing. He's shared on the following pages the same thoughts, stories, tips, and techniques in the same words that he's shared with me during many hours both on and off the water. Imagine, if you will, Captain Rick at the helm of his *Islamorada,* engine idling, his ever-present tall Mountain Dew in his hand, softly telling tales of his life on the water, eyes twinkling with humor and subsequently lit with angling passion. Take the time to read between the lines and you'll be surprised how he weaves angling tips and techniques into his stories. Tips on tides, structure, habitat, seasons, tackle, and more abound.

Reel Chance Fish Tales will take you out on the waters of Saint Helena and Port Royal Sounds, wind your way through the rivers of the famous ACE Basin, and allow you to share the experiences and universe of Captain Rick Percy. And put a smile on your face to boot . . .

Jim Goller
Executive Director, Hampton Wildlife Fund

Capt Rick

Introduction

As I sit here this morning, my mind is racing. This past Saturday I fished a charter with a young man named Dean Ray. Dean was diagnosed with cancer when he was thirty-five and beat it. His experience led him to write a book about his battle: how he overcame the odds and his beliefs that got him through the struggle. He gave me a copy, and I read it. I shared a few of my fishing stories with him, and he immediately urged me to write a book about my experiences as a fishing guide. I got to thinking about it and wondered what in the world I would write about. Slowly but surely, I reached back into my memory bank and started to recall many funny, exciting, scary, and unusual things that I had seen and been a part of on the waters of the Beaufort, South Carolina, area. How would I organize and relate some of those stories to perhaps put a smile on someone's face on a rainy day when fishing isn't an option? I wanted to share what I have learned about a sport that is enjoyed by millions of people and isn't restricted by age, race, gender, or health. Fishing is available to anyone who has the desire to enjoy some time outdoors on or near the water. If my experiences and limited expertise can brighten a day for someone or give them a better opportunity to catch a fish, then my time spent writing this is very worthwhile. I hope you enjoy reading it as much as I have enjoyed writing about my adventures and misadventures fishing in the Lowcountry. Time spent fishing is never counted against us. When I've passed to the other side, I hope my two daughters, Tani and Gwen, and their beautiful children, Andrea, John, Abbi, Jesse, and Jason, can read a passage and feel close to me again. It is for them that I write this book.

Chapter 1

The Early Years

Sitting on a low-water bridge on Deer Creek north of Iola, Kansas, I watched my grandmother, Pearl Pansy Percy, rear back and throw a big shiner minnow into the pool below us. She was using a short baitcasting rod and reel loaded with Dacron line, with a big red-and-white cork three feet above the hooked minnow. She handed the rod to me and told me to hold on tight. The cork danced around as the minnow tried desperately to free itself from the J-hook to which it was attached—but to no avail. Soon thereafter, the cork began moving off toward the middle of the creek and suddenly disappeared in the coffee-colored water. I reared back with all the might a four-year-old could muster and felt the rod throbbing. What a rush that was—one that I have never gotten over sixty-five years later. That first bluegill was the beginning of a lifelong addiction, one that would lead me to many wonderful destinations and give me the opportunity to establish friendships with an unbelievable number of people. I am forever grateful to both sets of my grandparents and to Mom and Dad for always including me whenever the chance arose for us to be together and enjoy the sport of fishing.

I was a freshwater fisherman for many years, living in the Midwest, after I graduated from college. I fished for everything you can imagine, including bass, stripers, walleyes, muskies, crappie, white bass, and catfish. The channel catfish in the Neosho River near Iola, Kansas, were always a favorite, as my grandfather Kenny Abell and I would wade the river to catch them. What a treat on a hot summer day to feel that cool river water swirling around your legs and the warm summer sun on your back.

My introduction to saltwater fishing began in Port Aransas, Texas, while on family vacations back in the middle 1970s. The area had two very long rock jetties guarding the entrance to the shipping channel and separating the beach from the deeper channel. We would buy live shrimp at a local bait shop and fish them under corks on the surf side, catching speckled sea trout, redfish, and sheepshead. I absolutely fell in love with that type of fishing. My chance to pursue it further came in 1990 when I was transferred by Dupont from North Dakota to South Carolina. I purchased a boat from Low Country Marine in Walterboro before I even closed on a house. It was a sixteen-foot McKee Craft, more of a river sled than a boat. The bow was absolutely flat, and it was built to fish rivers, not rough water. That provided some exciting days on Saint Helena Sound (more on that later). Every weekend found me in the

Ashepoo, Combahee, or Edisto Rivers, where they entered Saint Helena Sound. The area is known as the ACE Basin and is famous for its tannic acid rivers, which are often clear but have a very dark, almost black, coffee color. The name ACE derives from the first letter of each of the three rivers named previously. They are tidal and inhabited by many species of fish. The estuary system formed by these three rivers at the mouth of the sound is one of the largest on the Atlantic side of the country. As a result, our marine life is varied and plentiful, as you would expect.

In 1992, Jennie and I moved to Beaufort from Walterboro in order to be closer to the water. My job with Dupont as an agricultural chemical marketing representative allowed me to live wherever I wanted in my territory, since I traveled the whole state of South Carolina and the mountains of North Carolina. Jennie did all the legwork and found us a nice home in a great neighborhood that we both liked. Living in Beaufort opened up new waters for me, as it is strategically located between Saint Helena Sound and Port Royal Sound. I have access to both, via public landings, in a matter of minutes. The open ocean is only a fifteen-minute run from a number of my favorite landings. The waters in Port Royal Sound area are different from those of Saint Helena Sound. No freshwater rivers come into the Port Royal Sound area as they do on the Saint Helena side. The clarity and salinity are cleaner and higher respectively, especially in periods of rain events. I do have an affinity for cleaner water, as I believe it helps the bite, especially for species like sea trout that depend a lot more on seeing their prey than they do on sensory location.

Becoming a fishing guide had been on my radar for years and years. In 1962, when I was fourteen, I spent a week with my Uncle Gene, who was a schoolteacher in Branson, Missouri. That was long before Branson ever became famous for its tourist attractions and country music. It was just a sleepy little Ozark town built right on Table Rock Lake, above the dam, and close to Lake Taneycomo, formed by the water discharge below the dam. Since Gene had his summers off from school, he was a bass fishing guide on Table Rock Lake. He also fished for rainbow trout that were stocked in Taneycomo. He was everything I wanted to be when I grew up. I thought it must be the best job in the whole world: fishing and getting paid to do so. How could you do better than that in life? So the thought was deeply rooted in my limited memory bank for the next thirty-five years. One day, out of the blue, I decided that when I completed my career with Dupont, I would start a fishing charter business in Beaufort. As I looked into the requirements to become a licensed guide, it was obvious some advance planning was in order. You must have a USCG mariner's license to get a South Carolina state charter vessel license. This had several requirements, including 360 days at sea, plus passing the physical and taking the Coast Guard examination. I began keeping a daily log of all my outings to meet the days-at-sea requirement. I kept records of time on the water, tides, weather conditions, water temperatures, and fishing locations, as well as what I caught or didn't catch, and when and where in the stage of the tides. I named all my drops. A drop is a specific area where fish are caught on a fairly regular basis. A creek mouth with a particular oyster-shell outcrop may constitute a drop and thus have a name. South Point, Tennessee Hole, and Johnny's are all drops I currently fish. My log has over three hundred named drops that I am able to recall, plus some that I can't remember where they are located for the life of me. They cover the area from Twin Sisters at the mouth of the Ashepoo River, clear down to Skull Creek at Hilton Head Island. I have kept records since 1992 and still do so today. The historical information accumulated helps me decide where I might fish, at the very least in a general way. In 1997, I had enough time at sea to begin to pursue my captain's license. At night I attended Sea School, a preparatory course for the Coast Guard exam, for a month in Savannah, Georgia. I passed the exam that summer, along with the physical, and Reel Chance Charters, LLC was born. I was still twelve years away from retirement from Dupont, but my course was set. Since I was already fishing with my Dupont customers on a fairly regular basis, I decided to charter part-time until then, and I used weekends, holidays, and vacation time to fish thirty to forty charters a year.

Having passed the requirements and received my United States Coast Guard Mariner's Certificate, valid for five years, I was ready to begin chartering by the end of 1997. There are a lot of things to consider when starting this type of business. Legal issues were resolved by obtaining an attorney, who did the proper paperwork for the formation of the limited liability corporation and submitted the application to the state. Insurance was another factor to be reconciled. It was recommended that I carry no less than a million dollars of liability. There are not a lot of insurance companies that offer commercial insurance for fishing charters. I was able to get mine locally through an agency in Beaufort that was recommended to me by another guide. I applied to the South Carolina Department of Natural Resources (SCDNR) for my state charter license, issued not to the individual, but instead to the vessel. I've always had issues with this policy, as I believe the license should be designated to the captain, not the vessel, but I haven't made that sale to the SCDNR yet. A Coast Guard requirement to hold a captain's license includes belonging to a drug consortium, as random drug testing is mandatory. I joined the American Professional Captains Association out of Florida to be in compliance. As I planned to fish some offshore for cobia and black sea bass, I needed two different licenses from the NOAA, the federal watchdog. That pretty much rounded out the paperwork portion. The only other compliance was keeping my daily charter logs issued by the SCDNR and reporting them by the tenth of the following month. I was ready to go fishing.

Chapter 2

Boats

Boats—I love them. There is just something exhilarating about being on the water in a boat. As I mentioned earlier, a sixteen-foot McKee Craft was the boat I was fishing in when I decided to start guiding. It was a well-built, heavy fiberglass vessel with an Evinrude 88 for power, but looking back, it never really suited my needs. The draft was certainly shallow enough to get up on our mud flats to fish, but it was not very seaworthy in any type of rough water. It had a center console with no T-top, so it afforded no protection from the elements. The bow rode flat to the water and was fine on calm days. Rough water was another story. Two different instances come to mind that might clarify that a bit.

I invited a good friend of mine, Joe Blackwell, down to do some cobia fishing with me in Saint Helena Sound. Joe worked for an ag dealership in Pamplico, South Carolina. He and I hit it off from the time we met, and we became good friends through the years. One pretty May day, Joe took me up on my offer. We loaded the McKee and launched her from the public landing at Bennett's Point. A short fifteen-minute ride had us out in the mouth of the sound at a marker called the Light. The Light is located just southwest of Otter Island and sits on a mud flat. The western edge falls from five or six feet of water into thirty feet very quickly. It is along this ledge that cobia and other pelagic predators trap bait that moves with the tide. Schools of menhaden and mullet use this edge like you and I do the highway. I like to set up in around fifteen feet of water to cobia fish. After getting anchored, we set out several rods with cut bait, both mullet and shad, on the bottom. The water was absolutely beautiful when we set up, as smooth as glass. The clouds reflecting off the surface of the water was Mother Nature's painting at its finest.

After catching a couple of small Atlantic sharpnose sharks and having no cobia bites, we had a huge run on the port rod. Joe told me to grab it, and I did. I could barely pull it out of the rod holder, as whatever was on the other end had the rod tip pulled clear down to the water, and the fight was on. I thought for sure I had the world-record cobia hooked up. Immediately it became apparent that I could not turn the fish, and the reel was losing line so fast I knew it would spool me in short order. Joe grabbed the anchor line and hauled it in, stowed it, and cranked up the motor to give chase. I was fighting the fish from a seat up on the front deck of the boat, so Joe swung the bow to the southeast, toward the open ocean, and gave chase. I quickly started gaining line back and was relieved to see the spool on the reel start to fill again. As all this was transpiring, Mother Nature decided to throw her nickel's worth into the battle. The wind started to pick up, and the tide changed direction and began to ebb. Unfortunately, they were moving against each other. When this happens, the water starts to get angry. Whitecaps and two-to-three-foot seas appeared in what seemed like minutes. Meanwhile, whatever was on the other end of the line made steady headway toward the ocean, and in rougher water to boot. I hung on for dear life, as the fish was in total control. I began to notice that every time we went over the top of a wave and down into the trough, the next wave would break over the bow. I wasn't too concerned since the boat was foam filled and supposedly would not sink.

This scene played out for about another fifteen minutes, and Joe finally said in an extremely serious tone, "Ricky, we got to talk!" I turned around and looked at him in the cockpit and caught a glimpse of our forty-eight-quart cooler floating behind him. The cockpit had a foot of water in it. The boat was taking on water with every new wave. I told him to hang on a bit more, as I was really getting the fish close to the boat now and sure did want to at least see it. With a look of astonishment, he simply nodded back. Ten minutes later we got our first look at an absolutely giant hammerhead shark. I worked it up close to the boat to cut the leader as close to the hook as possible, and we were astonished to see how big it truly was. It used up every bit of twelve feet measured against that sixteen-foot boat. To this day, I have not caught another one that approached its size. After we released it, I grabbed a bucket to help the overworked bilge pump empty the water out of the boat. We turned her toward land and eased our way back. We now had a following sea to work with, and I was able to keep the bow up high enough to keep the oncoming waves from breaking over it. I know Joe was very happy to get his feet back on dry land. Both he and I have told this story umpteen times.

A peer of mine who worked for Dupont in the upper part of the state came down from Columbia on a Fourth of July weekend to try to fish some of our nearshore wrecks and reefs. The closest access to three of those reefs is from Russ Point Landing, which is on the Hunting Island side of Fripp Inlet. Jack Cullipher was an experienced offshore fisherman, so I wasn't too concerned about the National Weather Service forecast of two-foot seas. That was about the maximum wave height that I felt the McKee Craft could handle safely. If I had to pick one word to describe the run through the inlet into the ocean, it would be *dangerous*. The front of the inlet is loaded with sandbars that shift constantly, and the surf on the ocean side can be really ugly. The channel is fairly deep out to the bars, and as the tide moves the water in and out of the inlet, it is forced to narrow, which in turn causes the current to be very swift. It's not bad if the winds are calm or blowing in the same direction as the tide is running, but a wind blowing against the tide . . . now that's a horse of a different color. And that is what we ended up facing us as we neared the narrow part of the inlet. I decided, foolishly, to give it a go. As we entered the narrow portion of the channel, the waves increased dramatically in height. It took every bit of skill I could muster to keep from ramming the bow into the upcoming wave. At one point, the boat came completely out of the water, the prop spinning air as the wave we climbed fell out from under us. She slammed down and started up the next one. I knew better than to try to turn around and go back. Putting the vessel parallel to those five-foot waves would have been the kiss of death, as she likely would have rolled over, so I stayed the course and kept the bow up the best I could.

We finally got onto the bar and were able to get to the ocean side safely. The seas outside the inlet were not nearly as rough as they were in the entrance. Jack had been very quiet during the whole ordeal, which wasn't in line with his normal character. I acted like it was just a normal run, not letting him know that it had scared the tar out of me. It was a lesson that I've not forgotten, even in my bigger boats. Although the seas in the ocean were a little rougher than I wanted, I decided to go ahead and fish a while and let the tide flow out and perhaps settle the channel down a little bit before attempting to get back inside. Just outside the bar, I could see schools of menhaden flipping on the surface. I figured there might be spanish mackerel and bluefish working them, so we set out two trolling rods with Clark spoons behind the boat. I also had a big Pro Laser plug, and we ran that out with a light wire leader behind the boat. I trolled alongside the bar in about fifteen feet of water. We had put several Spanish mackerel in the ice chest when the big rod went off. The fish screamed a hundred yards of line off the reel in a matter of seconds. Jack grabbed it out of the rod holder, and I turned the boat to follow the fish. After a fifteen-minute fight, Jack slid a beautiful king mackerel up to the side of the boat, and I buried the gaff behind its head and hoisted it over the gunnel. The fish was so long we had to cut it in half to get it to fit in the ice chest. Thankfully, the inlet had calmed considerably for the run back to the landing. We weighed both halves of the king when we got home, and it was a twenty-six-pound fish. It was my first king mackerel, but that wasn't the luckiest part of the day, by any means.

I knew that the McKee Craft would not suffice to run charters. Three people trying to fish out of it was too many, and it wasn't enough boat to safely handle the style of fishing I wanted to do. Some guides prefer to stick with one type of fishing, such as those with smaller flats boats who do nothing but target redfish on the flats. I personally wanted the option of fishing the flats, fishing the big waters of the sounds, and also working the numerous nearshore reefs and wrecks that we have available to us. Trying to buy a boat that is capable of handling all those preferences is very difficult to find, believe me. A friend of mine, Captain Doug Gertis, had a prototype of a boat that Scout was going to build, called a 196 Sportfisherman. It was a hybrid flats boat and bay boat, over nineteen feet long. The deck areas on the bow and the rear were more than adequate to handle several fishermen. A center console and a poling platform rounded out the features I was looking for in a boat. It came equipped with a Yamaha 150 outboard motor. I bought one in the fall of 1997 and was ready to do business.

My very first charter is still vivid in my mind. I got a call from a couple staying at Hilton Head who had a fifteen-year-old son, and they wanted to catch a fish. I was so excited to be doing my first trip, but slowly the pressure started creeping up on me. The night before the trip, I barely slept. This was a part of the professional guide business that I hadn't thought of at all. I ran through my mind the game plan that would best fit the weather and tides. What if I couldn't find a fish? How would I ever justify charging someone a whole 250 dollars for a boat ride? And what fish should I target? It was early May, and I did have several options. I met Bob, Lynn, and their son, Charlie Burt, at the Chechessee Landing. They told me they didn't have a preference on what species to catch, so I took the easy road and went to a big sandbar near the number one marker off the north end of Hilton Head. We set up on the bar and fished with fresh shrimp on the bottom on the flooding tide. They caught a few small bluefish, which I cut up for bait. After hooking up several small sharks, Charlie hooked up with a five-foot blacktip shark. It put up a beautiful fight, with lots of jumps and long runs. They were all really excited over the catch, but not nearly as excited, and relieved, as I was. The pressure absolutely melted off my shoulders. Man, this was fun! Charlie wanted to keep the fish and have it mounted. When I told his mother the steps I would need to take to kill it, as in beating it to death with a billy club, she immediately opted to release the fish, and reluctantly Charlie gave in to Mom. The trip back to the landing was a great ride. I'll bet by the next week when Charlie was telling that story to friends back in Chicago, that shark was every bit a ten-footer.

Not all my early trips went exactly as planned. In that first year, I received a call from another guide and friend, Captain Thomas Maybank. Thomas was a very good fisherman and specialized in redfish. He fished out of a small Hewes flats boat and had a great reputation for catching fish. His only drawback was that he could only fish two clients comfortably, and he had a four-person trip coming up and needed another guide. I gladly accepted two of them to fish, as getting trips early on in the business wasn't very easy. We met them at the Sands Landing in Port Royal. Dr. Norm Baker, his two middle-aged sons, and his teenage grandson were eager to go fishing. Thomas put Norm and the grandson in his boat, and I got the two middle-aged sons. The first thing out of their mouths was, "We have to beat Dad whatever we do." Oh, brother! Thomas was tough to compete with. Both of us took off straight down the Beaufort River, and Thomas cut over to the flat on Parris Island Point. I went the other direction, to the big flat that guards Station Creek below Land's End. It always held several good schools of redfish and still does. The only limiting factor to fishing that flat on a falling tide is that the outside of the flat gets skinny first. In other words, one might get fooled into thinking there is still plenty of water to float the boat while fishing close to the oysters, when that may not be the case on the outside edge. Thomas told me later that when he saw me pull up on that flat, he thought I was either extremely gutsy or stupid. It turned out the latter was the case. With the tide half-gone, sight-fishing was just getting to that really great window of opportunity. Sure enough, as I poled in toward the shells, a big school of redfish sat up and pushed a wake a blind man could see. I had both men on the bow and had them cast. Those fish were absolutely aggravating. They would not eat for either love or money. They swam over, through, around, and in our baits for close to an hour, and they were big fish, likely in the twenty-eight- to thirty-inch range. It finally dawned on me that I had better pay attention to how much water I had left on the flat. I turned and looked back out to the river, and my stomach knotted. I could see little wavelets rolling over the sand on the outside edge. There was no way I could get my boat back across that bar, as the water was only four or five inches deep by then. Geez! I was like the rat in the trap: forget the cheese—just let me out of the trap. However, the chance to slip off that flat was long gone. I explained the situation to the clients, telling them it would be four hours or so before the water would come back in deep enough to get the boat to float. Reluctantly I called Thomas and told him the situation. He was able to get around the flat and up into Station Creek to pick us up. I walked the clients through the mud up onto the hill and around to his boat. As we waded the last several yards out, Norm, with a huge smile on his face, was busy with the camera. My boat was sitting high and dry by then, and I had put out the anchor. Six of us were a crowd in Thomas's small boat, so we ended the day and took them back to the landing. We didn't charge them, of course. I paid Thomas a hundred dollars to help make up for his loss that I had caused. About seven that evening, he ran me back down to my boat, and I took it home and cleaned it. I was really feeling down about the whole day, but it got worse. That night I had a kidney stone attack about midnight, and I spent the rest of the night in the emergency room. I lived through the stone, Thomas called me again in the future to do trips with him, and we fished that Baker crew a number of times through the years. They always asked me if they needed to bring waders. All's well that ends well, I guess.

I fished with the Scout until 2006, when I decided I wanted to upgrade to a little bigger boat. My neighbor's son, Freddie Rourk, was working at a boat dealership in Georgetown, South Carolina, selling Pathfinders. I went up and cut a deal to buy his demo. It was a twenty-two-foot Pathfinder Tournament series with a Yamaha 150 outboard. As soon as I got it home, I took it down to Savannah, Georgia, to have a custom T-top built. I elected to go with a hardtop that would hold my weight to stand on, and I had a ladder from the top secured to the rear deck. I was doing a lot of sight-fishing in the spring for cobia, and what a great advantage it was to stand up on the top and be able to see cruising fish at remarkable distances. The extra three feet of length is really significant in a boat, and fishing with four people was a lot easier than in the Scout. I also felt a little more secure when fishing the reefs nearshore, as the seas can change suddenly, and getting back safely was no longer an issue. She would run close to fifty miles per hour if I needed to get back in a hurry, and the seas allowed me to run that speed comfortably.

The hardtop turned out to be both a blessing and a curse. My number of cobia sightings while sight-fishing them in the Broad River increased dramatically. The height advantage was even greater than I had anticipated, as I was able to see a foot or two down into the water at much farther distances than simply standing on the deck. When the fishing gods smiled on us, the river was as slick as glass, and sight-fishing was at its best. I could see the telltale wake of a cruising fish at several hundred yards while standing on the hardtop. Even more significant was the opportunity to see fish in a chop, especially those hanging around weed lines that formed during periods of higher tides and were swimming a foot or two under the surface. Those fish gave off no visible signs of their presence on the surface and were pretty safe from predators like me, unless you had the height to see down into the water. That was the blessing. The curse? Being six feet above the back deck and keeping your balance was a circus act at times. My plan was that if I lost my balance, I would try to launch myself off the top to either the port or starboard side. That way the motor would miss me, and I would live to fish another day. A very good client, John

Sweetwood, from Atlanta, was fishing solo with me one day. John normally brought other fishermen with him, but he was by himself this particular day. We had been catching a few redfish, and as the tide turned to go out, the water got as slick as a baby's bottom. It was perfect conditions to catch ol' Mr. Cobia cruising on the surface and soaking up the rays. I had John go to the front deck with rod and reel in hand, and I crawled up the ladder onto the top. It wasn't very long until I saw a nice cobia crossing the front of the boat. I pointed out where John should make the cast, and he let fly. As they often will, the fish turned right toward the boat and was on a collision course with us. John's cast sailed past the fish, so I knew some quick action was needed to have another shot at the fish. I went to jump down to the first step of the ladder, and a severe pain ripped through me. I had pulled a hamstring muscle, my left leg collapsed, and off the ladder I went onto my back on the rear deck. Lying on my side, I pulled myself to the starboard gunnel and saw the fish sliding down the side of the boat directly toward me. I had an extra rod rigged sitting in the right rod holder with a large artificial shrimp tied onto the leader. I grabbed it out of the holder and dropped the bait right behind the boat while still lying on my side. *Kaboom!* The fish nailed the bait, and the rod bent double. I never got a chance to pass the rod to John, as the fish ran back under the boat and cut the line on the motor. It was game over before it hardly began. It took a couple of weeks to get over the muscle pull, and even longer to get over the vision of John standing on the front deck laughing at the whole situation. Looking back, I guess I was lucky that I hadn't fallen off that top any sooner than I did. I decided then and there that would be the last hardtop I would own, just to ensure that I didn't have a weak moment and crawl back on top.

I have been going out to Lake Charles, Louisiana, since 1994 to fish in Lake Calcasieu. It is an absolutely great place to fish for speckled trout, and the lake is known for its big trout. The biggest I have caught so far weighed in at six-and-a-half pounds, but there are trout there in the double digits. In 2010, we stayed at a fish camp and shared the camp with several guys from Louisiana who were good friends of our host, Toby McGowan. Toby was a peer of mine, as he was a Dupont salesman form Lafayette, Louisiana. One of the guys was Ken Naquin, who worked for Monsanto at the time, selling agricultural chemicals. He was also a big-time tournament fisherman and was sponsored by Lake & Bay, a well-known boat company. Ken had an almost brand-new 2010 Lake & Bay Backcountry 24, with only sixty hours on the 250 Yamaha motor. I was really smitten with how she looked sitting there in the camp and thought it was the nicest-looking boat I had ever seen. After I had pored over it, both inside and out, Ken told me he had a new one on order and was going to sell this one. The next day on the water, Ken found us, pulled up, and told me to get in and run her. Man, what a boat! She rode and handled like a dream, and I was amazed at the room the twenty-four feet produced. We talked about price a little, and after I got home, I couldn't get that boat off my mind. My Pathfinder had almost eight hundred hours on the motor and was four years old, and I was ready for a new ride. I sold it within a week of putting it on the market. Ken and I came to an agreement on price, and I met him with a check in Columbus, Georgia, and towed her home. It did not have a T-top, so I took it down to Savannah and had a custom top built. And no, it wasn't a hardtop. In the early summer of 2010, the *Reel Chance III* was ready to go to work. I absolutely loved that boat. It was the softest, driest ride I had ever encountered. My Pathfinder didn't hold a candle to the hull on the Lake & Bay. It floated every bit as shallowly, if not more so, as the Pathfinder, allowing me to get up skinny on the flats and chase the redfish. The Yamaha 250 top speed with a wide-open throttle was right at 55 miles per hour, and she got on plane quickly. Getting off the flats in shallow water was a snap, even with four clients in the boat. Nearshore wreck fishing was very comfortable, as the boat handled two- to three-foot seas with ease. It had a Minnkota Riptide trolling motor with I-pilot that made fishing the wrecks very easy. The I-pilot feature had an internal GPS with a spot-lock feature that allows the trolling motor to hold the boat in a specific spot, within a few feet, and thus negates the need to put down an anchor. Anchoring on a wreck can be a real pain in the butt, as the winds and current speed are constantly changing, and often anchor adjustments are required to stay within a few feet of where you need to be fishing. Just a few feet can mean the difference between being a hero or a zero on a wreck. I really like being a hero.

I retired from Dupont on December 31, 2010. I was very much geared to run my Reel Chance Charters business full-time. All the years of part-time guiding had given me a very large client pool. My repeat business was growing every year and was close to 50 percent of my business at that time. I hooked up with a website programmer out of Florida who built websites exclusively for fishing guides. Captain Josh Utsey, a good friend and guide in Beaufort, recommended Cyber Angler. Rudy Gomez owns and operates the business, and he went to work on my website. To be very honest, I wasn't impressed with the way it looked, but clients have told me over and over it is the best and most informative website of any of many in our area. I do a fishing report section and post the results from every trip I do, not just the good ones. I currently have around two thousand folks who follow my reports, with thirty-six thousand visits a year. I have no idea how that compares with other charter companies in the area, but it works for me, as I do all the trips I want every year and even slip a number to other guides.

I ran the Lake & Bay for five years. As I was approaching the one-thousand-hour mark on my motor and it was getting close to being out of warranty, I had a decision to make concerning either repowering the boat or moving on to another boat. The decision would have been easy if Lake & Bay had still been building boats, but they had gone out of business in the latter part of 2013 or early

2014. I looked at and researched a number of twenty-four-foot bay boats. After running the Lake & Bay, I was sure that it was the size vessel I needed, and it fit my business perfectly. There was a large number of bay boats on the market, but every single one had a feature or two I did not like. In the summer of 2014, I read that a guy named Tom Gordon had purchased the Lake & Bay hull molds. Tom worked for Hells Bay prior to starting on his own and was well known for his boatbuilding. I contacted him that fall and took a trip down to Florida to his shop to look at the boat firsthand. I wasn't disappointed. In fact, I was pretty amazed at the improvements he had made in a number of areas on the boat. The hull was exactly the same as my Lake & Bay, so I didn't even water test the boat. The wiring, console size, and hatch accessories were all improved, and the quality looked to be unsurpassed. We sat down and put together the *Reel Chance IV* on paper. It was loaded with great features to facilitate fishing. A Minnkota Riptide 112 trolling motor, custom T-top with rod holders, a livewell for bait, large release well, and two Yeti coolers were all part of the package. The real kicker was the motor. I told Tom I wanted another Yamaha 250 for power, and he went to work talking me into putting a Yamaha 300 on the transom. I doubted it would do all performance-wise that he was suggesting, but in reality it turned out it was even better. An AmeraTrail trailer went under the boat, and they brought it to me in March of 2015. I had a buyer waiting for the Lake & Bay, and it was gone the day the new boat got to the house. What a boat it is!

I wish I had a nickel for every time someone has walked up to me at the gas station as I filled it and said, "That is a beautiful boat." Not only is it a good-looking boat, but it is a fishing machine. I can easily handle four fishermen with the large bow and rear decking. The T-top is a bit of a hassle if all four are casting constantly, but we work around it fairly easily. The Yamaha 300 pops it out the water and puts it on plane with ease, and the ride is incredibly soft and dry. Running at 3500 RPMs, she burns about twelve gallons per hour and clicks along at 34 miles per hour. The wiring job is immaculate and easily accessed through a large hatch on the front of the console. The 102-inch beam allows her to float in shallow water, which is needed on low tides to catch redfish on the flats. She is a great boat to charter fish in our area, and I plan to keep her for a long time to come.

Reel Chance I

Reel Chance II

Reel Chance III

BOATS

Reel Chance IV

Chapter 3

Mama

I have had the opportunity to meet a lot of great folks while chartering. As you might expect, there are often times when things don't go exactly as planned or unusual things happen. I really enjoy having kids on the boat. Many have never been on a fishing charter, and it is an exciting adventure for them. Also, their expectations aren't generally as high as adults, so just getting bites and a pull from any size fish can make the day for them. To top it off, they do say the funniest things, always in dead seriousness. Several trips come to mind when I think of kids.

One May I had a call from a dad who had three sons he wanted to take fishing. The boys ranged in age from five to twelve years old. I was still fishing in the Scout at the time and made arrangements to meet them at the Broad River Bridge Landing. My game plan was to get them some bites early on and then maybe try to cobia fish toward the end of the half-day trip. We had an absolutely gorgeous day to fish. Light winds from the southeast with an incoming tide had the river as smooth as glass. I ran out to a big sandbar off the north end of Hilton Head Island in Port Royal Sound, and we set out bottom rigs with frozen shrimp and cut bait. Immediately the boys started catching fish. Atlantic sharpnose sharks, bonnethead sharks, whiting, bluefish, and a few Spanish mackerel were all on the menu. And gosh, do kids love sharks! It doesn't matter how big, they are just nuts to catch one. We stayed on the sandbar for several hours, and the boys were giving the fish a real thumping and having a great time doing it. As the tide began to slow down, I asked them if they wanted to spend a little time trying to catch a cobia. The river was in perfect condition to sight-fish them, and I felt our chances of seeing a fish on the surface were really good. They all agreed, so I pulled the anchor, and we headed the Scout back into the Broad River. We agreed that I would make the cast and hook the fish up if we saw one, and I would hand off the rod to the oldest boy. It wasn't fifteen minutes until I saw the telltale *V* that a pushing cobia makes on the surface. I eased the boat into position, jumped onto the bow, and let fly a cast past and in front of the cruising fish. I reeled the live menhaden quickly past the nose of the cobia and saw the fish turn toward the bait. I stopped reeling and felt the thump as the cobia grabbed the bait. Fish on! I handed the rod to the boy, and the battle began. It looked to be about a thirty-pounder, not huge, but just right for a twelve-year-old. He was able to work the fish in close to the boat, and then disaster. It ran under the boat, crossed the line over the motor prop, and cut the line. What a disappointment! It really took the wind out of the boy's sails. I told him not to worry, that we would find another one. I quickly retied the leader and hook, grabbed a bait from the livewell, and put the boat back in gear. Within literally seconds, I spotted a fish about seventy-five yards in front of the boat. We repeated the same scenario: the fish ate the bait, and the youngster was hooked up to another fish. This time all went as planned; they decided they would like to harvest the fish, so I buried the gaff and hoisted it over the gunnel. Lo and behold, there was the leader from the first encounter hanging out of the cobia's mouth. It was the same fish we had hooked originally. After several minutes of picture taking, wiping down the boat, and getting the fish on ice, we were ready to start looking again. I reached down and turned the key to crank the Yamaha 150, and nothing. She wouldn't turn over. I jumped back to the battery compartment and checked the wires and then tried to turn her over again. Nothing. She clicked a few times but wouldn't fire the motor. All eyes were on me now, as they waited anxiously to see what would happen. I simply looked up at them and said, "Well, boys, now what?" The five-year-old, without hesitation, looked me straight in the eyes and said, "Let's call Mama." I fell off the seat laughing. That was a young boy's solution at its best. Fortunately, a good friend of mine, Captain Danny Rourk, was coming down the river, so I waved him over and told him the problem. He jumped in the boat with me and got in the battery hatch, grabbed a pair of pliers, tightened the connections, and bingo—she fired right up. Ever since that day, whenever disaster looms imminent, I think of the logical solution: "Let's call Mama."

Joseph and Jaws

Chapter 4

A Pig

One of my peers in the ag business was Bennie Hughes from Ehrhardt, South Carolina. Bennie liked to fish and often brought customers to Beaufort to fish with me. On one particular trip, he decided to bring his grandson, Bryce, with him. Bryce was about five or six years old at the time. It was in May, and the cobia were thick in the Broad River, so we elected to anchor and try chumming one into the baits. We set up on a sandbar and had our baits soaking on the bottom in about fifteen feet of water. Cobia fishing can be very slow, to say the least. With large live greenback herring for bait, it is a waiting game to try to get that one special bite. When I first came to South Carolina, I stopped by a local tackle store to pick up the tackle I would need to try to catch my first cobia. I began to quiz the gentleman behind the counter on how to go about catching cobia and asked what was needed. An old man sitting in a chair by the counter looked up and without hesitation said, "Lotta chicken, lotta beer!" Of course, he was referring to the amount of time you had to put in to be successful, and he was spot-on. Patience is a top priority in being able to put a cobia in the boat. While waiting for one of the rods to bend over with the line screaming out, Bennie and I got into a discussion about some of the different things that folks do to try to get a cobia hooked up. One fellow I know who fishes Saint Helena Sound a lot has a big blow-up Turtle raft that he ties off behind his boat while he is fishing. Cobia are curious fish and like to have something to get under. More than once I have had them come to the surface and lie directly behind the boat. Another trick of the trade, if you are fortunate enough to catch a legal-size cobia, is to run a line through its mouth and tie it off to a cleat so that it is swimming next to the boat. I was telling Bennie and Bryce a story of a friend who had done exactly that after catching one the previous day. I repeated how he had said that after twenty minutes or so, they looked over the side and a real pig (meaning a very large cobia) was swimming next to the one they had tied off. Bryce, not catching the meaning, looked up at me with a total look of distrust and said, "How did that pig get in the water?" Of course, that brought the house down.

Broad River cobia

Chapter 5

Henry

I came to South Carolina in January of 1990. A week after my arrival, I had to work a trade show in Columbia, South Carolina. The very first person I met was a fellow named Henry Chaplin. Henry worked for a local distributor who handled my product line. He was a very direct individual, large in stature, and easy to get to know. Through the years, we became good friends. Henry casually mentioned to me one time that he thought fly-fishing might be a lot of fun and a challenge. That evening I ordered a fly rod and reel to get him started. He took to it immediately, practicing his casting every chance he got. He became fairly proficient at throwing the fly and started catching fish on a regular basis. A fifty-five-pound cobia on my boat was his largest fish, but his first love—and nemesis—was redfish. Henry went to the Bahamas and Belize several times and caught bonefish with success, but redfish was another story. He was snakebit when it came to catching redfish on the fly, not just in my boat, but anywhere else he went. The summer of his forty-eighth year, Henry started having stomach problems. Eventually they did a colonoscopy and discovered a large tumor. He went to the Mayo Clinic in Jacksonville, Florida, where they did exploratory surgery. They sewed him up and told him to go home and get his affairs in order.

The following January we had a two-week period of very nice weather, as a Bermuda high-pressure system had set in above us. Conditions were ideal to sight-fish redfish. On a whim, I called Henry on a Saturday evening and asked him if he felt up to giving the redfish a try the following morning. He said he would love to and climbed into my boat around eight the next morning. I ran to Parris Island Point and eased the boat up onto the flat. The tide was still easing out, but there was plenty of water to fish. Climbing up onto my poling platform, I looked around me, and what I saw was absolutely astonishing. In any direction I looked, I could see a school of redfish. The flat was absolutely covered with fish. I could easily see five hundred fish in the gin-clear water in schools of twenty to fifty fish each. I tied a Dahlberg Diver, a bulky topwater fly, on Henry's leader, and he made the cast to the closest school. Immediately a twenty-seven-inch redfish pounced on the fly; Henry set the hook, and the fight was on. What a beautiful fish it was, gleaming copper in the morning sun, as Henry held it up for a picture. For the next hour and a half, he had an absolute ball catching redfish. After the eighth fish, he looked up at me and said he needed to rest a bit. I suggested we just call it a morning, as I could see he was feeling weak, and he agreed. That was his last time fishing, as he passed away several months later. At the reception after the funeral, his family had set up a few pictures on a table. In the middle of them was the one of Henry holding that beautiful fish on that lovely January day. I often reflect on that day and look skyward with a grin, as I know Henry is looking down with a grin on his face too. The good Lord blessed us that day, for sure.

Nice pair of reds

Chapter 6

Storms

Fishing in South Carolina coastal waters can have some challenges once in a while. Navigating the sounds and rivers requires some care and knowledge, as they are full of mud flats and sandbars, and seeing a boat stranded in shallow waters is not uncommon. With seven-plus-foot tides being average, and extreme changes of even nine feet every six and a half hours or so, the opportunity to run aground is a constant threat. Nonetheless, very seldom are these circumstances life threatening. Storms, on the other hand, can very well be just that dangerous. Today's electronics, including smartphones, give access to instant weather conditions and can keep a mariner on top of the situation. Even then, judgment comes into play, and one does not always make the most prudent decision. I certainly have become more conservative in my thinking as I've gotten older, and I do everything I can to stay out of harm's way, but I still have gotten myself into situations that I wish I had not.

One of those times included my grandsons John, Jesse, and Jason. They live in Seattle, and I try to have them stay with us for a week or so every summer. All three absolutely love to fish and spend time on the boat. Several years ago, while I still had the Pathfinder, we decided to spend some time fishing in Saint Helena Sound. One unique feature of the sound is the opportunity to find some really nice shark's teeth on a couple of small spoil islands that show during periods of lower tides. These small mounds of rock and shells are located on a mud flat close to Brickyard Point and are well known to produce a large number of shark's teeth. That, of course, is right up those boys' alley. The only catch is that toward the bottom of the tide, the water can get too shallow to float the boat. When that happens, you simply have to wait for the tide to turn and come back in until you have enough water to get off the flat. This particular day we started on the teeth-hunting expedition as the water was falling out. We had pretty good luck finding some nice ones, but I made the mistake of not watching the water level as closely as I should have. It was a very warm summer's day, and I was paying attention to clouds building over Otter Island. It wasn't long before we could see some lightning in the clouds, and as they continued to build, I knew it was time for us to head back to the landing at Lucy Creek. Even though the storm was building to the east of us, I didn't feel comfortable with the conditions. I had waited too long, and the boat wouldn't budge. The bow was down in the mud, and there just wasn't enough water to float it off the flat. I tried cranking the motor to back us down, but it was so shallow I couldn't get the prop down to get a good-enough bite to pull us out. All four of us climbed out and into the mud, trying to shove her off, but to no avail. Our only option was to sit and watch that storm build and hope the water came back fairly quickly, as the tide had turned and was starting to rise. We sat in the boat and watched the storm move inland and then turn and head in our direction. We could see the rain falling like a curtain across the sound, and flashes of lightning were beginning to pop with increased frequency. I had my eye on a certain oyster that was showing, and I knew when it was covered with water, we could slip the boat off the mound and head for the landing.

By this time, the boys were starting to get a little nervous about the whole situation, and I was too, as I knew it was going to be close. Fortunately, the incoming tide beat the storm. With one mighty heave, the four of us were able to shove the boat backward into enough water to float her. Believe me, the cheer that went up from those three boys could be heard clear back to Seattle. We eased off that flat, put her on plane, and made a mad dash for the hill. As I was tying the boat off to the dock, the skies unloaded on us with a torrential downpour. I got a little wet, to say the least, putting the boat on the trailer, but I was very glad to have the boys safe in the truck. I'm sure that is a memory they will carry with them for the rest of their lives. I know I will.

I have been in several storms inland and never been overly concerned about my safety, until one July day in 2015. I had a charter trip scheduled with a client from Hilton Head and planned on a Pinckney Landing pickup. To keep from getting mixed up in all the traffic on Hilton Head, I chose to launch at Lemon Island, make the run down the Chechessee River to Port Royal Sound, and cut through Mackay Creek to the landing. Total running time at 35 knots is about thirty minutes from landing to landing, and the scenery on the river is a lot prettier than on the highway, anyway. The weather forecasters had a 30 percent chance of precipitation for our area that day, with the highest chances later in the afternoon. That is a fairly common forecast for a summer day in lower South Carolina. Things didn't start off very well that morning. I was a little ahead of schedule and was getting ready to make a cast or two at a good-looking spot in Mackay Creek when my phone rang. I reached up and picked it up off the console, and somehow it flipped out of my hand. I made a swipe to grab it and knocked it over the gunnel into twenty-five feet of water. Geez! What a lousy way to start the day. I went on to the dock and picked up the client. I had been fishing Dawes Island recently and had a school of redfish pretty well dialed in, so we headed back out Mackay and straight across the river to Dawes Island, which separates the Broad River from the Chechessee River. We picked at the fish a little up and down the shells. I noticed a rather dark cloud building up over Bay Point and Saint Phillips Island. It got darker and darker, and soon I could see signs of a thunderstorm. We were located almost due west of the storm, and almost all of our weather moves to the east. The storm started to intensify, and I watched it as it actually moved to the north, over Saint Helena Island and up toward Port Royal and Parris Island. At this point, I could see it was more than just a little cell. Even though we still had a couple of hours left on the trip, I didn't feel comfortable. I elected to head back to the landing and drop off my client. My concerns were growing as I headed the boat back toward the sound in Mackay Creek to try to make the run to Lemon Island Landing and my truck. Now it looked as if the storm had changed direction and was moving directly toward me across the Broad River. When I hit the mouth of Mackay and looked out across the river, I knew I was about to be in some trouble. The sound was frothing with foam on top of the waves as the wind battered it. It hit me like a train going 50 miles per hour. The winds jumped from 15 knots to gusts of over 40 in a matter of seconds. The rain came blowing sideways. But the worst by far was the lightning. Never in my life, before or since, have I seen the frequency or intensity of lightning and thunder that was in that storm. It cracked over my head and put the fear of God in me. The sky was as black as night, and it was so low I felt like I could reach up and touch it. For a few seconds, panic had me. I shook it off and thought about what I needed to do. The boat was pitching around in five-foot seas in the creek, and it was raining so hard I could not see twenty yards ahead. I decided the first step was to get a life jacket. I did and attached it to the console tubing. Why I didn't put it on is beyond me, and it is a question I have asked myself often. As Forrest Gump said, "Stupid is as stupid does." I wanted out of that boat and into some kind of shelter. The closest place to find shelter was the landing I had just left. I turned the boat around and headed back at the safest speed I could run, as visibility was horrible. I finally got to the landing and somehow got the boat secured safely with enough line so it wouldn't smash to pieces on the dock. I crawled under a palmetto tree at the top of the landing, and there I stayed for the next forty-five minutes as the storm raged over me, right down Mackay Creek and into Calibogue Sound. I was cold and as wet as a drowned rat, but I thanked God for seeing me through that mess. The outcome could have been very serious. As soon as the storm passed, I made my way back to Lemon Island with no further problems but certainly more respect for Mother Nature.

John, Jason, and Jesse

Chapter 7

Kersplash!

One drizzly December day, I called a close friend of mine, Jim Goller, to see if he wanted to jump in the boat with me and give the fish a try. Jim does all my electronics work on my boat, and he and I try to fish together whenever we can. The skies were overcast with an intermittent drizzle, and the air temperature was in the mid-fifties. The water temperatures were in that same range, and the bite had been pretty good. I was still running my Pathfinder at the time, so we hooked it up to the truck and ran to the Broad River Landing. The water was very clear, with a nice low tide. We went to a bank we call Bluecoat, eased the trolling motor over the side, and slid the boat into two feet of water. It wasn't long until we started putting the redfish into the boat. Working our way slowly down the bank, we caught a number of redfish. Most were in the slot. The slot for redfish in South Carolina is fifteen to twenty-three inches. Only fish that measure between the two may be legally harvested, while any that are under or over must be released. Several were in the twenty-six-inch range, which weighs in around seven pounds or so. I was standing on the very tip of the bow, working the trolling motor, which had a steering handle. I never saw the shell before the prop banged it, and the boat came to sudden halt. Unfortunately, I didn't. I lost my balance and could feel myself getting ready to go overboard. I fought it as hard as I could by putting a death grip on the rubber handle on the steering tiller. It was too late, as the rubber grip came off the handle and overboard I went, landing fully face down in that cold water. Cold water filled my rain bibs and soaked me to the bone. I jumped up and crawled back into the boat. Later on Jim remarked that it took me a lot less time to get back into the boat than it did to go out. He asked me if I was okay, and I assured him there was nothing hurt but my pride. We decided that was enough fishing for the day, as I was starting to shiver and ready to get out of the wet clothes. I fired up the Yamaha and pointed the bow back up the river toward the landing. Jim was sitting next to me, and on the ride back, every few minutes he would erupt with a burst of laughter. It wasn't quite as funny to me as it was to him, but if the shoe had been on the other foot, I would have been doing exactly the same. I knew that story would be all over town in short order, so I went ahead and posted it in my website fishing reports. I got a lot of comments from my website readers about the incident, as you might imagine.

A year or so later, Jim called me one evening and 'fessed up, telling me he had taken a dip that day. It seems he had run his boat to the Edisto Island marina to do some repair work on a customer's boat, and as he was docking, he lost his balance and fell into fourteen feet of water. His hat floated off, and he had to swim to get the boat and secure it. I immediately called a mutual friend, Johnny Ulmer, and related the story. Johnny enlisted the help of his secretary, whom Jim did not know, and had her call Jim and inquire whether he was giving scuba diving lessons, as her family was coming to Edisto Island for a vacation and would like to hire him for a diving charter. He told her, in a rather cold tone that she was confused; he was not a scuba diving guide, and she should look elsewhere. It took him several hours, but as he thought about it, he finally started putting the pieces together and knew that we were putting one over on him. It's a long road that doesn't have a curve in it!

In late January of 2017, I received a call from a very close friend who had been our neighbor in Sigourney, Iowa, back in the early eighties. Dick Morse lived half a mile west of our little farm, and we became very good friends, hunting and fishing together during the six years we lived in Iowa. I hadn't seen or talked to him in thirty years, other than trading Christmas cards, and was thrilled to hear from him. He and his wife, Merla, had a trip planned to visit relatives in Florida and wanted to stop and visit a day or two. We confirmed the dates, and they arrived on schedule. Dick had not fished in salt water before, so I was anxious to show him what a great fishery we had here in Beaufort. We loaded the boat the next morning, which dawned clear and cold. I decided to try to put him on a redfish to start the day, then switch to trout, which were still biting in the deep creek holes. I ran up to a favorite drop for the tide we had and set the Power-Pole down in six feet of water. We both made casts up into the grass, hoping a redfish might find the mud minnows we were using for bait. I was standing on the bow, and Dick was next to the console. He had reeled in to make another cast, and somehow the rod slipped out of his hands as he made the cast. What happened next took only four or five seconds, but it looked like a slow-motion film. He reached over the gunnel as the rod was sinking, lost his balance, and the next moment both legs were pointing skyward. Over he went, headfirst into the cold water. When he popped up, he had a hold on the boat with his left hand, and the rod gripped in his right hand. I grabbed him, took the rod, and was able to hoist him by the seat of his britches back over the gunnel and into the boat. He was a drowned rat, as you might imagine. I always keep some sort of spare clothes on the boat, so he stripped off and put on a pair of rain bibs and a shirt. I asked him whether he wanted to go back to the house, but he just grinned and said heck no, he had come to fish. That is just what we did, and we did pretty darn well, catching trout in a deep creek. We both got lots of laughs out of that morning and had a great visit to boot.

Chapter 8

Dolphin

Our estuary system provides great habitat for the bottlenose dolphin. Most of us older folks remember the TV series *Flipper*, and the star of the show, a bottlenose dolphin. I hear many people refer to them as porpoises, but they are dolphins and year-round residents. The sounds and rivers here in the Lowcountry of South Carolina are loaded with all types of bait fish, including mullet and menhaden, greenback herring, and a number of species of fish that sustain our dolphin population. Shrimp, both white and brown, are abundant through much of the year, and I doubt a dolphin would turn down a shrimp. I won't either. Sea trout and redfish are right on the top of their menu. As our water tends to get colder in the late fall, we start to lose a lot of the bait as it moves south to warmer waters, and it is then that the dolphins really turn to redfish—and the redfish know it, too. They tend to school in large numbers in the winter and stay up very shallowly on our mud flats. It is simply a game of "I hope he eats you and not me." Twice

I have witnessed dolphins herding a school of five- to seven-pound reds, pushing the fish up onto a dead oyster shell, and then going out of the water on their sides to grab one of the flopping redfish. It is really something to see. Of course, if you were looking to try to catch one of those fish, you might as well find greener pastures. I have had two memorable incidents involving dolphins.

The first involved a good friend of mine, Johnny Ulmer, from Ehrhardt, South Carolina. Johnny was an ag customer of mine, and we hit it off from the very start. We hunted and fished together through the years and made a number of trips to Louisiana to chase redfish and sea trout. You couldn't ask for a better partner than Johnny. He came down to Beaufort to fish with me one day and brought a friend of his, Mickey Jones. It was in the winter, and we were pretty much limited to fishing for redfish, as the trout weren't on the bite. We had a nice tide to work with that day, with a higher mean low, which kept the water on the flats a little longer. Tides, both high and low, are stated in average mean. Tide charts give the variance for each tide daily at a given location at a given time of day. Full and new moon tides are usually more extreme than waxing or waning moon tides. One might see a high tide of +1.0 feet on a tide chart. This simply means the water will be one foot higher for that particular tide than the average mean. Low tide variances work the same way. We had worked pretty hard at finding fish most of the morning, and we had moved several times. I decided to give the east side of the river a try and ran across to one of my favorite areas. As we approached the bank, I noticed two dolphins working along the edge of the oyster shell I wanted to fish. They just went back and forth along the outside edge of the shell, as there wasn't enough water on top to support them. However, there was enough water to support a redfish, and the top of the shell was loaded with a very nice school of big fish. They obviously had no intentions of leaving the safety of that shallow water and were very aware of the presence of the dolphins. I eased the boat down to within casting range, and Johnny and Mickey put the baits in perfect position. Immediately they were both hooked up to very nice over-the-slot reds. Those darn fish stayed right there, and we worked them over for quite some time, catching fifteen or sixteen off that shell. The dolphins had cruised on down the bank as we approached, but I know without a doubt, they were the reason for our success. That was one of the few times I've seen them as a positive when trying to catch fish.

My most unusual dolphin encounter came in January of one particular year. Never have I seen a dolphin take a hooked fish or had a dolphin bite a bait of any kind. On this particular day, I was fishing alone on the Saint Helena Sound side and had moved into a creek between two islands. The water was very clear, as it often is during our colder winter months. I was looking for sea trout and was in a creek that had downed timber along the edges and on the bottom. The water was about twelve feet deep, and the tide falling out slowly. I like to throw a soft plastic grub on a jig head for trout in situations like that. The one I was throwing that day was a green/silver with a curly tail, and I was working it very slowly, bouncing it off the bottom and letting it fall back down. I had hooked and released five or six trout, when I had a bite that felt exactly like a trout. I set the hook, and the whole world exploded ten feet in front of the boat. Out of the water shot a very large dolphin, and I watched with a wide-open mouth as it threw the hook. I was absolutely stunned. It all happened in just a matter of seconds. My thought was that as I picked up the jig, I accidentally set the hook in the dolphin, and it reacted. I was glad to see it headed back down the creek. After resting the water a bit to let everything calm down, I resumed fishing in the same spot. With the second cast I made, I felt the familiar thump on the rod of a trout bite, and I set the hook. Unbelievably, another dolphin shot out of the water, but this one didn't throw the hook. It took off like a nuclear submarine down that creek, and the line was screaming off my spinning reel. It took less time than it took to write this sentence before it was all over. I was standing there dumbfounded, staring at an empty reel, not believing what I had just seen. To this day, I have never had it happen again. My only regret is that I didn't have someone with me to witness it.

Andrea's redfish

Jesse nice redfish

John shark

Jason's jack crevalle

Abbi's Redfish

Chapter 9

The Emory Professor

I am now in my twenty-first year of guiding. In those years, I am "guesstimating" I have fished somewhere close to thirty-five hundred or so people. Many of those have become good friends and repeat clients. It is really amazing that out of that many folks, I can honestly say that there are only a handful or less that I wouldn't want back on my boat. One that stands out in my mind was in my earlier years when I was still fishing the Scout. I got a call from a lady from Atlanta, and she said that she and her husband were coming to Hilton Head for a vacation and wanted to book a fishing charter. I could tell by her voice and the questions she asked that she might not be the outdoorsy type. We agreed on a date, and I was sitting in the boat at the landing at the agreed-upon time. They came down the ramp to the boat, and they were an older couple; the lady looking rather frail. I could tell this trip wasn't likely her idea or cup of tea, but she was obviously being a sport about it to please her husband. It turned out he was a professor at Emory

The Emory Professor

University in Atlanta. They got on the boat, and we took off to look for redfish. I had a very nice school of fish I had been working that week, but the tide was a little too high when we started, so I ran to a grass edge to start off the trip. I had live shrimp in the boat and hooked them up under a popping cork; then I tossed them to the grass edge, handing a rod to each of them. He immediately started giving her instructions on all phases of fishing. Shortly her cork went down, and she was a little slow to react and missed the fish. He acted like it was the end of the world. She sat quietly and let him run his mouth, and I chimed in and told her not to worry about it because we would get more bites. However, the way he was treating her and his tone of his voice were really ugly. I decided I would fix his wagon. As the tide finally got right, I ran down to the drop I knew the fish would be on. It was a small live oyster shell surrounded by grass, and the fish loved to lie on top of the shell once it was covered with enough water. They were really good fish, averaging twenty-five to twenty-eight inches, or around six to eight pounds. I set the anchor within a good casting distance and moved the lady to a front pole seat that was on the bow deck. I instructed him to fish off the back deck, and I cast his bait as far away from that shell as I could throw it. I picked up her rod, pitched the bait over the shell, and handed it to her. No sooner did the cork hit the water than it disappeared. The rod bent double, the line peeled off the drag, and she had the first smile I had seen on her face all day. I did the supervising as he watched from the back in silence. I slid the net under that eight-pound redfish, and it was game on after that. After the fourth fish she put into the boat, he asked me if maybe he ought to cast his bait in the same spot. I told him no, that his was where I wanted it, and the fish would show up there sooner or later. And by golly, he actually did catch one there, but by then she had eight nice redfish and was chattering like a child with a new toy. That was how we ended up the day: lady 8, professor 1. I don't believe he tipped me.

Chapter 10

From a Zero to a Hero

A very good friend of mine, Junior Justice and his wife Kathy, from Hendersonville, North Carolina, like to come down and fish with me in early October, which is Kathy's birthday celebration. That timing is normally really good fishing, as we have a number of options to choose from as far as the type of fishing that is available. Of course, it is weather and tide dependent and can be either fabulous or frustrating. We have had both types of trips through the years. The options we have allow us to fish for a variety of species. The breeder redfish, often weighing between twenty and forty pounds, are in the Port Royal Sound area. The school redfish and sea trout are working over the white shrimp and mullet as they exit the estuary, so that bite is generally excellent. Outside the beach, the nearshore wrecks and reefs are starting to really turn on with black drum, sheepshead, weakfish, bluefish, and spanish mackerel. On one trip I recall in particular, we had started inside, trying to find some redfish on the flats without much luck. Two friends of mine, Captain Danny Rourk and Captain Chris Mattson, were both on the Parris Island Reef, working the bull reds over pretty good. "Bulls" is the nickname used to identify the large breeder redfish that come in from the ocean to spawn. The tide was running out perfectly, with the water glassy. The only issue I had was bait. I had run to the Dawes Island bank but just couldn't find the menhaden or mullet I wanted to use because that is what the bulls were really feeding on at the time. I did have plenty of cut menhaden with me that I had caught earlier in the summer and put up in the freezer, so I decided it would work and ran to the reef. I slid the boat between Danny and Chris, as they were quite a distance apart. Both had clients hooked up to fish when I got there, so my confidence was pretty high that we would have Kathy with a rod bent over shortly. I put out the baits and we waited . . . and waited. Nothing. Meanwhile, both my buddies were wearing them out. Chris called me on the phone and told me to slide on down closer to him, as they were getting double and triple hookups. I set the boat thirty yards above his and put out the baits, with the exact same results. Not a bite. Geez. This was starting to get frustrating. Chris called me again and told me to slide on down and he would give me his spot, as they were through for the day. Not only did he give me his spot, but he gave me a dozen live mullet, which is what he was using for bait. I set the anchor exactly where he had been sitting, rebaited with the live mullet, put them on the bottom, . . . and we never got a single bite. I was sick to my stomach. Those fish had obviously moved. Junior was starting to pick at me about it pretty good, and I certainly had it coming. We sat there for half an hour with zero action, until I couldn't take it anymore. I told them to reel them up, as we were going to find something else to catch. I was feeling the pressure and was pretty embarrassed, to say the least. The winds that day were calm, and the water as smooth as a baby's bottom. On a whim, I headed the boat toward the ocean and a big sandbar a couple of miles offshore. We made the run out of the sound between Bay Point and the north end of Hilton Head Island, and I had the ears laid back on the Lake & Bay, as the seas were beautiful. The sandbar that parallels the shipping channel on the east side runs out from Bay Point for almost two miles. At the very end of the bar, it turns from the south to due east and extends for quite a distance. The water on top of the bar is roughly seven to eight feet deep at high tide, and the bar falls off into twenty feet of water on the ocean side. Bait fish of all kinds stack up on top of the bar, and the predators cruise the edges, waiting for them. As I neared the outer end of the bar, I saw exactly what I was looking for—birds, and lots of them. Terns, gulls, and even pelicans were working and diving on the bait that the fish below were pushing to the surface. We could see a number of different schools of fish, making the water boil as they tore through those bait schools. My favorite tactic for those fish is to use a bucktail jig in a three-fourths-ounce size and either cast into the schools, or, if I have novices on the boat, troll through them. The secret to making the bucktail work is to trim off the tail just behind the hook. This imitates the exact size of the bait fish that are being consumed. We targeted a group of working fish and trolled through them. Kathy was immediately hooked up to something good. The fish was smoking line off the reel like it wasn't even hooked. She worked hard and after a bit had a false albacore next to the boat. These are fish that are very prevalent off the North Carolina coast, but seldom do I catch them here. They are absolutely one of the most powerful fish you will hook for their size. This one probably was close to the six- or seven-pound range, and it put up a terrific fight. They also caught several bluefish and a couple of nice Spanish mackerel to round out the day. At least, I saved a little face.

A good False Albacore

A pretty spanish mackerel

Chapter 11

Brays Island Tournament

Brays Island is a very nice, upper-class residential community. It is located off the Pocotaligo River, north of the end of the Broad River. It is an outdoorsy-type community, with hunting, fishing, shooting sports, and equine activities available to residents. They have their own landing and docks located on Haulover Creek, with nice facilities. I have fished with quite a number of the owners through the years and have gotten to know quite a few people there. I was hooked up for a short time when I first started guiding with Captain Thomas Maybank. Thomas was a very energetic and competent guide. He was one of the best redfish guides working our area and an excellent entrepreneur to boot. He helped start an annual redfish tournament that was open to residents and guests of Brays Island, which, of course, put him in contact with a large group of folks who liked to catch redfish. Through the years, the tournament grew to the point we had to go outside to Charleston to enlist extra guides, as there were not enough local guides to accommodate the number of folks who wanted to fish. Brays would put on a very nice supper the night before the tournament, and the two-person fishing teams would draw for guides. Total inches caught determined winners. It was always a fun day to fish, and I enjoyed the competition and was fortunate enough to get into the winner's circle a time or two. One particular trip in that tournament stands out in my mind above all the rest, hands down.

Through the years, for various reasons, the number of folks who signed up to fish dwindled. Rather than have a drawing for guides, they let the fishing teams contact and hire the guides prior to the tournament. In 2014, I got a call from Larry Foster, asking if I had the date of the tournament open, saying that he and his wife, Diana, were signed up to fish the tournament. I did have it available, booked them, and told them that I would see them at the gazebo, the launching point, on the tournament day. Captain Bryan Freeman, a good friend and the in-house guide for Brays, called me a few days ahead of the tournament and told me about a spot where he was catching tons of bait shrimp, only needing a couple of casts with the net to fill the baitwell. I decided to catch bait that morning early, as the spot was very close to the tournament launch and would save me a buck or two to boot. I launched that morning from Gray's Hill Landing in the dark and made the twenty-minute run up the river to Bryan's shrimp drop. I threw the net three times and soon couldn't get another shrimp into the well. They were absolutely thick and nice-sized baits, perfect for redfishing. About the time I was putting the last of the shrimp into the baitwell, I saw Captain Danny Rourk pull into a cove below me, obviously to try to catch shrimp also. As I had far more than I would ever use, I decided to just slip on down and give him a mess and save him some time and trouble. As I eased the boat down the river and made a turn toward his boat, I ran aground on a sandbar that I obviously didn't know was there. I made the mistake of trying to turn out toward the middle of the river, not knowing the bar moved in that direction and the water was even more shallow. I had the motor jacked up on the Lake & Bay as high as it would go with the prop still getting a bite, but I succeeded in doing nothing but driving it higher on the bar and flinging mud all over me and the boat. What a mess! Here it was dead low, and I was looking at being stuck for an hour and a half or so, with the tournament launch only a half hour off. I was absolutely furious with myself. How could I be so stupid? Meanwhile, Danny had heard and seen all the commotion and was easing up as close as he could get to me from the middle of the river. I was only thirty feet or so from deep water, so we tied a line off his boat to mine to try to pull her off, but she wouldn't budge. I threw the anchor out and waded back to Danny's boat, and we headed to the launch. I was a mess: mud from head to toe and madder than a hornet at my stupidity. There were lots of grins as folks climbed into their boats to launch. Larry and Diana were being very good sports about it, and we climbed into the Brays Island deck boat, which hauled us back to my boat to wait out the tide. An hour later we finally got enough water to float it off the bar, and then we got loaded up and headed out. I had planned to start at an island tree drop in the Whale Branch and decided to try it, even though I liked the lower tide we should have had to start. I eased the boat into position, set the Power-Pole, put a big pretty shrimp on a circle hook, and cast it into the hole. I handed the rod to Diana and turned to get Larry going. Before I could pull his rod from the holder, Diana let out a yell, and her rod was bent double. She slid a very nice upper-slot redfish into the net, and we were on the board. I guess the good Lord was taking pity on me that morning, as she and Larry put twenty-three redfish in the boat at that tree. We had well over four hundred inches of fish, and they had lost a couple at the boat on top of the twenty-three they had caught, releasing everything. I knew we were in the running for top honors, but you never know in this game. We left the tree after the fish finally slowed down and quit biting, and we ran to another drop up the Pocataligo River. We didn't catch any more redfish, but Larry caught three very nice trout, which we put in the cooler to clean for their supper. To top off the day, we won the tournament. They each got several nice prizes, and the jabs I was getting earlier from my peers weren't nearly as painful.

Andrea and Abbi

A beautiful seatrout

A nice wreck flounder

Chapter 12

My First, and Last, King Mackerel Charter

One late fall several years back, I fished with a couple of guys from the Pee Dee area of South Carolina. We had a very good day on trout and redfish, in both quantity and quality. One of the gentlemen got to quizzing me about fishing for king mackerel off the coast and said he really wanted to give that a try. I told him that summer was likely his best bet to catch one, and he went to work on talking me into taking him and his girlfriend out on a charter to try to catch a few. I explained I did not normally run off the coast as far as would be required to get into the kings, and I did not run charters specifically targeting them. I was running the Lake & Bay 24 at the time, and since it held a hundred gallons of fuel, I had plenty of range to give it a try. If the seas were right, the boat was plenty safe to make the trip. He kept after me most of the day about setting up a trip, and thinking I would never hear from him again, I told him to give me a call in early summer and we would try to put a trip together.

My First, And Last, King Mackerel Charter

Lo and behold, the next June I got a call from him. He was all fired up to give it a go, and after trying unsuccessfully to persuade him to find an outside guide, I decided, *What the heck? I'll give it a try.* We set a date for early July. I needed a boat service the first week of July, and my mechanic, Trae Everett, happens to be a very good king mackerel fisherman. In fact, he has won a number of tournaments fishing for them. While he was working on my motor at the house, I mentioned I had committed to a king trip and was wondering if he could give me any pointers to increase my odds of catching a few. He immediately offered to let me use his king rods, and he also did the unthinkable, offering his GPS numbers for his spots. Of course, I jumped on both offers. Since I planned to launch from Russ Point Landing in Fripp Inlet, we made plans to meet at 5:00 A.M. at a gas station that was right on my way and close to his shop. The morning of the trip, I was up and at it by 3:30 A.M. I was greeted by a loud rumble of thunder, as a storm was passing over the top of Beaufort. I looked at the radar and forecast on the computer and saw it would be out to sea by 6:00 A.M., which was our departure time. Hopefully, it would move fast enough to be out of our way before the trip. The rest of the forecast for the day looked good, with two-foot seas, which would be very doable for the fifteen-mile run. As planned, Trae was at the station when I pulled in at five. We threw the four rods he had rigged for me into my boat, and he climbed in and switched out the memory card in my Garmin GPS with a card that now had not only all my old numbers, but all of his. He threatened me with my life to safeguard his numbers, and I assured him only God and I would ever see them. I had just finished launching the boat and tying her off to the dock when my clients arrived. As it was still fairly dark, the lightning in the thunderstorm that was off to the east shone pretty bright and of course sparked a conversation about whether we could still go. I told them we had to catch bait out in front of Hunting Island, and that would kill more time and allow the storm to move past. Safety is always on my mind, and if I had any doubts, I would simply cancel the offshore trip and spend the morning fishing inside the inlet. Running through the inlet, I could feel the swells from the ocean, and after we crossed the surf line and turned north toward the beach, the seas were two to three feet. That is plenty safe to work with, but it does give the boat a little rock-and-roll motion. I expected the seas to quiet down even more as the day wore on and the tide slowed. Immediately I saw a pelican dive a hundred yards off the beach and knew he was catching what I wanted to catch too—menhaden, king mackerel candy. I ran toward the bird and saw the telltale flips on the ocean surface. Two casts with my eight-foot castnet and we had my big release well chock-full of perfect choker pogies. Things were really starting to come together, and I was starting to get excited about putting a big smoker king in the boat. Trae had shown me the numbers I needed to try and recommended I stop at the 6HI reef if the water temperature was around 78 or 79 degrees. The client asked his girlfriend whether she felt okay about going, and she said she was fine, so I pointed the bow to the open ocean and off we went. Since

My First, And Last, King Mackerel Charter

the seas were still fairly choppy, with only a short interval behind the storm, I could only make about 18 knots comfortably. Several times on the way out, the man leaned over behind me to ask his girlfriend how she was doing. She told him "just fine" each time, and that she was actually enjoying the ride. Arriving at the buoy that marked the reef, the water temperature showed 79 degrees on the GPS. Perfect, and to boot, the seas were starting to calm down, with just a two-foot swell to work the baits through. I went to work rigging the baits and staggered them behind the boat, with the last one being in the prop wash of the Yamaha 250. I noticed the client had gotten pretty quiet for a guy who liked to talk. I eased the throttle in and out of gear and kept my eye on the rods. Looking back toward the bow, I saw him on his knees, leaning over the gunnel, losing his breakfast. He finally got up and sat on the center console seat, telling me he was having a reaction to the Dramamine he had taken earlier and needed to get back to his truck. Now I have heard every excuse you can imagine why someone is getting seasick, but that was a first and really took the cake. Here it was, barely 7:00 A.M., and I was going to have to run back in and cancel the day. I was a little put out, to say the least. I began reeling in the baits and stowing the rods, when I glanced to the side of the boat and saw a fin protruding out of the surface. Spadefish! A whole school had come to the surface, as the cannonball jellyfish were pretty thick, and spadefish love them. After getting the last rod in the boat, I asked him if he could hang on for a couple of minutes to see if we could get the young lady hooked up on a spadefish. He agreed, with a reluctant tone, and I went to work to rig a light spinning rod with a light wire circle hook. I dipped out a passing jelly ball, cut a small piece off, and pitched it in front of a feeding spade. Handing the woman the rod, I instructed her to simply hold on until the rod was bent double and then to start reeling. She did exactly as told and was soon fast to a really big spadefish, around seven or eight pounds. And do spadefish ever fight! Catching one is like trying to reel in a swimming manhole cover, as they lie on their sides and pull. With lots of squealing and laughing, she got the fish next to the boat, and I slipped the net under the fish. Without asking permission, I rebaited and tossed the bait to another fish, and the scene was repeated. Miraculously, the man was getting better by the second, and after her fifth fish, he asked if he could have a rod. I rigged him up, and he joined the battle. Those fish stayed with us for an hour, and I don't know how many they caught, but we did keep eight or nine, as they are excellent table fare. After the fish went back down and the action slowed, I wanted to go on out to the king numbers, but the man said he would rather not and wanted to know if there were any other spots to fish on the way back in to land. I took them to the wreck of the *Savannah*, close to Hunting Island, and they caught a number of species, including bluefish, ladyfish, jack crevalle, weakfish, and a few flounder that they kept. We called it a day about noon, ran the inlet back to the landing, and unloaded. I decided then and there that was my last king trip, and I have been true to my word. If I ever catch one on a charter, it will be by accident.

My First, And Last, King Mackerel Charter

A Big Bull Red

Black drum

Chapter 13

One Hook, Three Fish

A peer of mine who was in our development group called one day and booked a late May trip with me. He was bringing a couple who worked for the University of Georgia Agriculture Department, and they wanted to try to catch a cobia. We had a beautiful day to give it a try, as the winds were light from the southeast, and combined with an incoming tide, the waters were smooth and clean. I decided to give the rocks in the mouth of Port Royal Sound a try. The rocks are old ballast rocks that the old-time ships dumped before picking up their cargo to haul back across the ocean. They are covered with live bottom and make a great habitat for all kinds of fish, from black sea bass to tarpon. Fishing for cobia can be a slow process. I had caught live menhaden, locally known as "cobia candy," prior to the trip, and I felt pretty good about our chances to hook up a cobia. I got the boat positioned properly, set the anchor, and put out four big choker menhaden on the bottom in thirty-five feet of water. I try to keep my clients busy while waiting on the

One Hook, Three Fish

big bite by letting them fish with cut shrimp on the bottom with light tackle. Black sea bass, bluefish, jack crevalle, and whiting are common catches off the rocks with cut shrimp. I rigged up three rods, all in the seven-foot medium-light category, and had them fishing on the bottom in no time. Several nice black sea bass had been put into the boat when the lady told me she was hung up in the rocks. She said she thought she had a bite, but the hook was hung up when she tried to set it. I took the rod from her to see if I could flip it out of the rocks and immediately felt a slight tugging on the end of the line. I figured a fish had eaten the shrimp and then gotten into the rocks before she could get it started up. I gave the line some slack to give the fish a chance to swim out of wherever it was hiding, and it did. I felt it come loose, but immediately a sharp thump, followed by a doubled-over rod, let me know that something else had taken the fish she had hooked. I handed her the rod back, and the fight was on. The fish was peeling drag off the small reel like crazy, the rod tip was almost to the water, and the woman was squealing that she needed help. She handed the rod to her husband, and he took over the battle. After several minutes, I could see some color in the clear water down the line, so I thought he had the fish almost to the surface. However, there wasn't just one fish close to the surface, but two. One was a black sea bass about fourteen inches long, and the other was a blacktip shark that had the sea bass in its mouth. The strange thing was the line still extended down into the depths below both fish. There was a third fish on that line that was working like crazy to get rid of the hook in its mouth. The sea bass had obviously eaten the shrimp, and when I pulled him out of the rocks, a big fish had grabbed him and gotten hooked. The sea bass had come off the hook but still had the line through its lips and was unable to escape. The sea bass was then grabbed by the shark as it rode up the line. When the shark was close enough to the surface, I gave him a good whack on the head with my gaff and he turned loose of the bass. The client went to work on the hooked fish, and before long a beautiful cobia came up to the top. It made several more long deep runs before I was able to put the gaff in the fish, and we had a thirty-four-pound cobia flipping in the bottom of the boat. After a lot of grins and high fives, we had the cobia in the cooler, and a pretty cool story to tell. I got a nice tip to finish off a great day.

An ocean Cobia

Chapter 14

Big Trout

My favorite fish to fish for and for table fare is, hands down, the speckled trout. They are locally known as winter trout, and our estuary system can be great for catching them. Unfortunately, we are right on the line where winter kill is always an issue. Trout can tolerate water temperatures in the high forties, but if they slip below that for any length of time, our fish are susceptible to massive die-offs. I have talked to South Carolina Department of Natural Resources officers who have seen the bottom of our waters literally covered with dead trout after an extreme cold spell. We can lose as much as 90 percent of our population because of winter kill. This, of course, really puts a hurting on our trout fishing for the following couple of years. I also think this is part of the reason we don't see as many "gator" trout caught here in our waters as they do in other, milder areas of the country, but once in a while we do catch some nice-sized trout. A six-pound trout here in the Lowcountry draws attention. My biggest trout to date was around six-and-a-half pounds, and I am always looking to try to break that seven-pound mark. Normally, these fish are loners. The smaller fish, up to around twenty inches, are usually schooled up, and one bite often leads to many. Only once in my twenty-seven years of fishing for trout here have I gotten on a school of big fish.

It was the middle of July, and hot as the devil. Water temperatures were in the mid- to upper-eighties, and a high-pressure system had settled in over the southeast coast for several days. It was not exactly what you would call prime conditions to catch trout. I had a charter with three gentlemen from upstate, and we started early to beat the heat. The trip went fairly well, as I started on a small flood tide on the tip of Dawes Island. The water was coming in that clear, green color we love to see, and I had a baitwell full of shrimp and finger mullet. They caught about a dozen or so fish, including several keeper trout, a redfish or two, and a couple of big ladyfish. It was not a gangbuster trip, but certainly not a bust, by any means. But things were about to change. As the end of our trip was nearing, I elected to make a run back toward the landing where we had launched and make one more stop on the point of a big creek that runs off the Beaufort River. Lots of oyster shell formed a nice rip that I liked to fish on the incoming tide, and catching a mixed bag there was the norm. As I neared the point, I noticed another boat sitting around the corner from where I liked to fish. It was a red Maverick, and I knew immediately it was Captain Doug Gertis, who was a long-time guide in Beaufort, South Carolina. I had hired him several times when I first came to the Lowcountry to entertain clients, and we became good friends. I really don't believe I have ever met anyone who loved to fish as much as Doug did. Numerous times I saw him, on a day when he didn't have a charter, standing on a bank somewhere trying to catch fish. He was absolutely addicted to catching fish. I eased my boat onto the drop around the corner from where he was sitting and dropped the anchor. No sooner than I had started to put the rods out, I saw him waving at me to come toward him. I eased the anchor back into the boat, put the trolling motor in gear, and slid around the corner toward him. He shouted to pull up and tie to the inside off his boat. I did just that, and he reached over and opened his cooler lid. What I saw almost made my eyes pop out. Stacked like cordwood were ten—which was the limit—of the most beautiful big trout I had seen since moving to South Carolina. He asked if I had any finger mullet and told me to strip off everything on the line except for the hook. I did as he said and hooked up a big finger mullet to the small circle hook. The tide was still running in and moving along a grass edge over a hard broken shell bottom. I pitched the first bait into the current along that grass edge, and instantly the rod bent double. I handed it to one of my clients, and soon a twenty-six-inch trout, weighing a little over six pounds, lay flopping on the back deck. Unbelievable— it was the middle of the afternoon on a hot July day, and the big trout were in five feet of water. We sat there, and I had my clients take turns working those mullet along that edge, with a bite on almost every cast. Doug sat on his poling platform, smoking a cigar and enjoying the show. We had put nine in the boat when one of the fellows said,

"Well, it's twenty after two; I guess we need to pack it up and go." I couldn't believe what I had just heard. Here we were on the biggest school trout I had ever seen, and he wanted to leave. All of the fish were between twenty-three and twenty-six inches long. Never before or since have I seen that size of fish schooled up, and they would eat only a free-lined mullet. Reluctantly I packed everything away, and we headed back to the hill. That was probably fifteen years ago, and believe me, I have tried that same scenario, with the same tide, more times than I can count. Yes, I have caught a few nice fish off that grass line, but absolutely nothing close to what we did that July day. Doug has since passed away, but I still marvel that he was kind enough to wave me in on those fish. Not many other folks would have been so generous. Thank you, Doug.

Vudu shrimp trout

Chapter 15

Jaws

One pretty summer day, I was out on the Broad River goofing off and looking for some new fish. I fish the creek at Generals Landing a lot in the winter but not much in the summer, so I decided to go poke around in the back of the creek and see what I could find. The entrance to the creek mouth is guarded by a large shallow sand flat that requires one to pay attention on low water to access the creek and not run aground trying to gain access. The channel that goes in from the river is on the north side of the entrance, but for some reason my mind wasn't exactly on my business that morning, and I got too far to the south side and ran the boat aground on that sandbar. As I had been running on plane, I was too far up the bar to even think about getting out and trying to pull it off. To make things worse, the tide still had an hour or more to go out, so I knew I was in for at least a three-hour wait to get the boat afloat again. I picked up my phone and gave Captain Danny Rourk a call, hoping by chance he was in the Broad too and didn't have a trip. Luckily that was the case, and within a matter of minutes, I saw him heading my way. I threw the anchor out on the Scout, grabbed a rod, and waded out to his boat. Of course, he had a big grin on his face. He was scouting and goofing off just as I was, so it looked like it would work out perfectly: fish a few hours, then run back and get my boat. He turned the bow to the north, and we ran up to a big flat on a favorite bank. The water by then was almost dead low, and it was very skinny on that flat. We both saw the redfish at the same time, pushing wakes close to the shells. They were too far to cast to, so I announced I was going to wade to them and see if I could get them to eat. I eased over the side of gunnel as Danny sat on his poling platform and watched the show. This particular flat is hard bottom, so wading is an option, whereas many of our flats are fluff mud and not good for wading. I eased along toward the fish, shuffling my feet as I went to keep from stepping on a stingray, and saw a really big bonnethead shark working along the same bank as the redfish. These are inshore sharks that we catch with regularity, and they eat shrimp, mullet, and crabs. I had no concerns whatever about sharing water space with it, as they rarely get over twenty-five pounds and aren't considered aggressive or any kind of threat. One does need to be careful when removing a hook from them, as they do have a mouthful of razors. I was keeping my eyes on the redfish getting closer and closer to casting distance, when I noticed the bonnethead had turned off the bank and was heading directly toward me. Still no worries on my end—I would just scare it off if it looked like a collision was going to occur. By now the shark was closing pretty quickly, so I stopped and waited for it to get into smacking range with my rod. When it was about six feet from me and still closing, I gave it a good whack on the head with my rod. Water flew everywhere, and to my surprise, that shark lifted its head out of the water and kept coming, teeth showing and shaking its head from side to side, like it was some kind of a mad dog. I was in full reverse gear, flailing away with my fishing rod, trying to keep it at arm's length. Somehow I kept from falling over backwards, and after a few seconds that seemed like hours, the shark dropped the attack and went on about its business. Danny took in the whole show and said it was quite a sight to see. I was just glad to get away from it, and I have certainly had a little more respect for bonnetheads ever since.

Jason's bonnethead

Chapter 16

The Law

Spending as many days on the water as I do, it is inevitable that I will be stopped by the local South Carolina Department of Natural Resources officers, or game wardens. Through the years, I have been checked numerous times, as their job is to protect our fishery resources and ensure that boaters have the proper safety equipment on board. I have absolutely no qualms about being checked, whether for safety equipment, license requirements, or for the fish that I keep for clients. In twenty-five years of fishing, I had never had any type of citation, as I was very careful to make sure that I was within regulations—and there are many, believe me. Each species has its own set of regulations, including size and number that may be kept. In South Carolina, it is illegal for a charter guide to have his personal limit of fish on board while chartering. The rules and regulations change on a fairly regular basis, so it is the responsibility of a charter captain to stay up-to-date on seasons, limits, and size restrictions. Through the years, I have gotten

The Law

to know many of the wardens who work our area. One in particular checked me numerous times with no infractions and finally got to the point where he would simply ask me if I was catching any fish when he pulled up next to me. He has a reputation for being fair but also pretty darn strict when it comes to the law. One fall day a couple of years ago, I had three guys on the boat from North Carolina, one of them a very good friend who was a highway patrolman. The day had been pretty darn slow, as the tides were fairly big and the water dirty inside the sound. We had three redfish in the livewell, all just barely over the legal size limit of fifteen inches, but all certainly legal. As the morning wore on, the winds calmed down to nothing, and I elected to run outside the sound to my beach numbers off Hilton Head to see whether there was anything biting on a small reef. We picked up a few trash fish and a couple of small sea bass, which we released. The ocean was really pretty, so I thought, *What the heck?* and we took off farther offshore to the wreck of the *General Gordon*. Once there we immediately started catching weakfish. Weakfish are pretty closely related to spotted sea trout and are not found much farther south than our area. The limits had just been reduced that year from ten fish per person to one, with a twelve-inch minimum, since the populations north of us had been on the decline. I had the limit in the livewell in no time, and we kept catching them and releasing them. We were the only boat on the wreck that morning, and looking toward Edisto Island, I saw a boat running directly toward us. When it grew closer,

I recognized it as the Contender that the wardens ran. I wasn't concerned in the least and had no reason to be. All was in order—or so I thought. When they pulled up next to us, I recognized the older warden I had known for years. He had two younger guys on the boat with him, whom I had not seen or met before. We greeted each other by name, and he asked me if I was doing any good, if I had any fish on board. I said we were doing pretty well at the moment, and I had three weakfish and three redfish in the livewell. He got a funny look on his face and asked if they could see the fish. I said sure, and one of the younger guys climbed on board. I opened the livewell, and he asked to see the smallest redfish, which I pulled out for him to measure. It wasn't much over the legal line, but it was legal. The older warden then asked me if I knew where I was. I said, "Of course, the *General Gordon*."

He replied, "Do you know how far offshore you are?"

Now I was starting to get an uneasy feeling. I said, "Not really. I guess three miles or so."

He asked me to get into his boat, and he pointed to a line on his GPS. It was the three-mile line, and we were six-tenths of a mile past that line, which meant we were in federal waters, not state waters. The next words out of his mouth hit me like I had been kicked in the belly: "Do you know that it is illegal to possess redfish in federal waters?" I looked at him, dumbfounded. I had totally forgotten that regulation, as catching legal-sized redfish that far out just never happened. The only redfish you catch that far out are the big breeders, and you always have to release them. Federal waters meant a federal offense. I could have thrown up. All the blood drained from my face, and I weakly answered that I had totally forgotten that and never gave the redfish I had in the livewell a second thought. He asked me for all my license information, which I handed to one of the younger wardens, who had a ticket book in his hand. The thought racing through my mind was, *What is the penalty for this infraction? Loss of charter vessel license? Confiscate my boat?* I was sure there would be a stiff monetary fine, but losing my license would have been crushing, to say the least. The warden began filling out the ticket, using my current license, and finally turned to the older warden and said, "What do I put down in section 216?" The response was "FW." It hit me like a ton of bricks—FW was for "federal warning." I looked at him and said thank you. He replied that he knew I was just ignorant of the law, as I could have easily released those fish over the side before they ever got to me. He also knew I had not caught them in federal waters, as that size fish is always inshore. I asked what he wanted me to do with the fish, and he told me nothing, just to get my butt back inside the three-mile line. And brother, did I! I know for certain that had he not been on board, I likely would have paid the price. The Good Lord was looking out for me that day, for sure. You can bet you will never find a redfish in my boat across that line again.

Chapter 17

Oops!

The laws in South Carolina state that it is illegal to clean or mutilate a fish in any manner while still on the water. That means you cannot clean a fish in your boat, even if you are tied up to a dock. Unfortunately, Beaufort County has not seen a need to build any fish-cleaning stations at any of our public landings, so cleaning fish for clients is a challenge. Many of the guides do not include fish cleaning with their services, but I always do if the clients ask me to do so for them. I keep bags on the boat for the fillets and have extra ice in the cooler to get them to where they are going. I normally carry a fish cooler on the boat with me to ice down the fish we are keeping, and I use it to clean the fish on if they are not too big. Otherwise, I just lay them out on the back deck after pulling the boat out of the water and fillet them there. A number of years ago, I had a couple of clients out of Hilton Head who wanted to catch a cobia. Back then it was pretty easy to catch one, as our population was excellent. We spent the morning sight-fishing for cruising cobia and ended up catching several. They wanted to keep one to eat, as many people really enjoy cobia steaks on the grill. I had them meet me at the Lemon Island Landing on the Chechessee River, since it is the closest landing to Hilton Head that is still easily accessible to the Broad River, where we do our cobia fishing. Returning after the trip, I put the boat on the trailer and pulled it out of the river and off to the side of the landing. As the fish was in the thirty-pound range and around thirty-eight inches long, cleaning it on top of the cooler wasn't practical, so I just laid it out on the very rear of the back deck. Grabbing my fillet knife, I looked up and saw two young game wardens approaching us. They had seen me lay out the fish and wanted a closer look. Both had on very nice white, short-sleeved button-up shirts with the DNR logo on the pockets. I hadn't met either one of them before, so I introduced myself as I sat on the back deck. The younger of the two was really interested in the fish and walked up and leaned up against the transom to get a closer look. We started talking about cobia and how the fishing had been. They could easily see the fish was well over the legal minimum size and never asked to measure it. One of my clients asked if I could tell whether the fish was a male or female. I remarked I couldn't by sight, but could tell if it had roe. I reached over and squeezed down hard on the cobia's belly, not noticing it was pointed toward the transom. To my amazement and horror, a brilliant blue stream of milt shot out of the fish and absolutely covered the left side of that young warden's pretty white shirt. For those who might not know, milt is the seminal fluid that contains the sperm that a male fish extrudes over the eggs that a female lays. That is how fertilization occurs. The milt of a cobia is as pretty a bright-blue color as you have ever seen. I was stunned, and the warden just stared at me, like he couldn't believe what I had just done. Dead silence prevailed momentarily, and then the other warden broke out in laughter. Not being able to help myself, I did too. By then, the young warden was trying to wipe the milt off, but it was far too late, as the stain was already soaked into the shirt. I grabbed a clean towel I had in the boat and threw it to him, but it was useless, as the damage was done. Looking up at my client who had asked the question, I simply said, "Male." Of course, that provoked more bursts of laughter from everyone—except the victim. He was finally starting to see a little bit of humor in the moment and told his peer he needed to find some reason to write me a ticket. Again, more laughter. They departed shortly thereafter, and I broke out in laughter for several days every time I thought about the incident. I'm sure even he finds it funny now. Sometimes in life you just have to roll with the punches.

Chapter 18

Divine Intervention

I received a call one day from a lady in Savannah, Georgia, who wanted to set up a cobia fishing trip. It was early spring, and the cobia were starting to show in catchable numbers in Broad River and Port Royal Sound. I told her I would be happy to fish with her crew, which included her husband and their priest. They had attended the same Catholic church in Savannah for twenty-five years, where they had been married by this priest. She mentioned he was an avid fisherman, and they wanted to treat him to a cobia fishing trip. We set up the day and time, and I was sitting in my boat waiting for them to arrive on the appointed day. Much to my chagrin, the water looked awful. We had a full-moon tide, which was rather extreme, and it had the water a muddy, chocolate-brown color—not what one would choose to sight-fish for cobia. I was convinced I had better have another choice to offer to them, as this just wouldn't work. The winds that day were light and variable; the water, flat and calm. After getting them situated on the boat, I explained the dilemma and offered several options. One was to run out to the nearshore reefs and wrecks, where the water was likely cleaner and yielded a better bet to see a cobia than in the river. They were certainly disappointed in my assessment but agreed to give the outside a try. We ran out the mouth of the sound to the wreck of the *General Gordon*. Very seldom can one not find something to bite at the *Gordon*, and this day was no exception; it was loaded with bluefish, black sea bass, and weakfish. I was hoping we might have a cobia come to the surface somewhere, since the water was a little cleaner, but that was not the case. We spent most of the morning on the wreck, and they had a good time with all the fish they caught. With time running out on the half-day charter, I called lines in, and we headed for the landing. The closer we got to the mouth of the sound, the dirtier the water became. I was running about 30 knots and keeping my eyes open for anything that might even resemble a cobia, but I was positive there was no way I would ever see one. Suddenly something dark caught my eye, and lo and behold, there was a cobia. It was cruising right on the surface, which is the only reason I was able to see it. It was gone from sight in a matter of seconds. My clients were all seated forward of the console, so I knew there was no time to try to get them a rod, point out the fish, and have them make the cast. Instead, I pulled the throttle back, grabbed the rod that was rigged with a large orange swimming jig, and made a long cast in the direction I had seen the fish. I reeled the jig for a short period and then let it sink for several seconds. Popping the rod tip, I danced the jig up and down for a minute and then felt the familiar thump as the cobia ate the jig. I slammed the hook home as hard as I could and handed the rod to the priest. I couldn't believe what had just happened. The odds of seeing a fish in that dirty water were less than winning the lottery. The priest did a great job fighting the fish, and I used the BogaGrip to secure him at boat-side. A BogaGrip simply clamps onto a fish's lip and allows an angler to release a fish unharmed. I knew the fish was close to the legal limit of thirty-three inches, measured at the fork of the tail, but I didn't want to gaff a fish that might be short of legal size. This fish measured thirty-two inches. After a number of pictures and high fives, I revived and released the fish. Even though it was short of legal, there were smiles all around, as it was the priest's first cobia. I looked him right in the eyes and told him that was divine intervention at its best. He grinned and said it may well have been just that.

Trophy sheepshead

Chapter 19

Baits

Fishing in our area is open to a wide variety of baits and tackle, and lots of different techniques meet with success. As a guide, it is my responsibility to get clients as many bites as I possibly can, and through the years, I've tried a number of different baits, tackle, and techniques. The ones I am going to describe, I have found to work the best for my situation. That certainly doesn't mean they are the best for you, as there are many fishermen in the Lowcountry who are very good fishermen and catch fish on a regular basis using totally different systems. Having said that, I hope you will find a nugget in here somewhere that will help you catch more.

There are a number of baits that work day in and day out. Live shrimp are hard to beat for the sheer number of bites. They are not always available, depending on the season, but everything in our system will eat a shrimp. Even me. There are a number of ways to fish with them, and I am generally speaking of targeting redfish and speckled trout, which are our most sought-after species inshore. If I am fishing with live shrimp in water six feet deep or less, I like to fish with them under a popping cork. I use a cork from Midcoast Products called an Evolution, which I really like for several reasons. First of all, it is weighted on the bottom. Many of my clients are not serious fishermen, and the added weight helps them cast farther, especially on windy days when we are fishing near a lee bank that requires a cast into the wind. Second, it pops very easily. Popping a cork simulates the sound of a fish feeding on the surface and will draw fish to your bait. "Thou who poppeth catcheth." Sea trout are especially susceptible to come running to a popping cork. A big advantage I see to a popping cork is the ability to present the shrimp in the right place where you think fish are staging, without getting hung up in shells. Much of our fishing is done using the current to move the bait along the grass edges over and around oyster shell mounds and in the back eddies where fish like to lie and ambush bait. I use a monofilament leader under my corks, usually around twenty-four to thirty inches long, and I like Trilene Big Game in thirty-pound test for most situations. If the water gets crystal clear, then I drop down to twenty-five pound test or may even go to fifteen-pound fluorocarbon. The latter is expensive, and I think the Trilene works very well in most situations. Drifting a live shrimp under the popping cork will catch just about anything that swims in our waters. I can't think of a single species that won't eat a shrimp, and that can't be said for a lot of the other live bait options. Sometimes it is too effective if pinfish, small croakers, and other "trash" fish are abundant. When I get in this situation, I will either switch out to mud minnows or finger mullet or suspend an artificial shrimp under the cork. Having to rebait hooks constantly from small fish biting is a pain and cuts down on the time you have a good bait in the water. Mud minnows are the easiest live bait to get, especially in the colder months, and therefore we use them a lot. Redfish, trout, and flounder all like them, sometimes as well as live shrimp. Finger mullets are also an excellent bait and will catch most inshore species. They are very plentiful in the rivers and creeks from midsummer on through the fall, and I like to fish with them live under a popping cork. I know a number of guides who fish with mullet exclusively, normally cut mullet fished on the bottom, and do quite well. They will set the rods in rod holders and wait for the bite before the client touches the rod. I fish this way once in a great while, but I find many of my clients like to have a rod in their hands most of the time, as it makes them feel more like they are fishing. Another good bait, especially for the big redfish in the fall, the ones we call bull reds, is blue crabs. Black drum and bonnethead sharks are also especially fond of half a blue crab fished on the bottom. Crabs quartered up are also very effective on the flats for school redfish, but I don't have easy access to them, and they are expensive, so I rarely use them except when fishing for bulls.

Several situations call for fishing baits on the bottom. Once the water I am working is much more than six feet deep, I generally switch out the popping cork rigs for some sort of bottom rig. I use a couple of different types of bottom rigs, depending on the speed of the current and the depth I'm fishing. My favorite bottom rig is a very simple one made up of a foot or so of thirty-pound mono leader tied to my main braided line with a surgeon's knot. I then attach an unpainted one-fourth-ounce jig head with a loop knot. This rig can be used with multiple baits and in a number of manners. If on deeper bottoms where the jig head is heavy enough to stay down in the current, I may well let it lie still, especially if I am fishing structure, such as a downed tree in the water. If I am fishing it in a faster current, I like to cast up current and let the bait sink to the bottom, and either bounce it along or just reel very slowly until I know it is past me and no longer able to stay on the bottom. I use all the live baits I've mentioned above in combination with the jig head and have had very good results on redfish, flounder, and sea trout with this method. If I happen to get on a good bite, say, of sea trout, then I might switch from the live bait to a soft plastic on the same jig head. I have three soft plastics that I really like to fish. The first is a Norton Sand Eel, Jr. It is a three-inch straight plastic bait with very little action, except for what you give it. This bait is super in deep creeks in cold water, as I work it slowly on the bottom, bouncing it up a foot or so, then letting it settle back down before bumping it again. Most of the time, the fish will hit the bait as it is falling, so line management is critical to knowing when you are getting a bite. Keeping in contact with the bait through feel is the key to catching a lot of fish with this bait. Lots of folks wave a rod around like they are in a sword fight, and I guarantee they miss a lot more fish than they ever catch, as they often don't have a clue they even had a bite. You have to focus on the bait to catch fish this way. To compensate, lots of fishermen use curly-tail plastics and cast them and just reel them back. This technique works fine if you are in a good school of feeding fish, but not nearly as well as the bottom-bumping technique in colder water when fish are slow to take bait. I also have been throwing a MirrOLure Lil John, which is another straight plastic soft bait. It is a little bit longer than the Norton, and also scented. I really like the "Blue Moon" color, or "Opening Night" in cleaner water. I typically try to stay with the old adage to fish clearer baits in clear water and darker baits in more colored water. The last soft plastic I use, and probably use the most, is the Vudu Shrimp by Egret Baits. It is an extremely effective shrimp imitation. There are quite a number of shrimp imitators on the market today. I have fished with a lot of them, and in my opinion, none will produce as consistently as the Vudu. I particularly like the clear gold flake in the 3.5 inch with the rattle. I fish with this bait under a popping cork and get really good results, and I have done great throwing it tight lined with just a mono leader. It is a super bait to fish deeper water and will catch a wide variety of fish. Even the blacktip sharks will eat it—and usually keep it. The key to catching fish on it under the popping cork is to be aggressive with your popping. Also, moving current really adds to success.

My favorite way to fish, without a doubt, is throwing topwater plugs. I don't do much of this on my charters, as I'm always concerned about people whizzing all those treble hooks past other folks' heads—including mine, maybe especially mine! So I'm usually alone on a scouting trip or with a friend or two when I fish with topwater. There are several myths that go with catching fish on top. One is that you have to have low light, such as dawn or dusk, to be productive. Wrong. All you need is the right action on the bait above a fish that is hungry. The other myth is to use smaller topwater baits. Wrong. I throw the Super Spook most of the time. It is a big bait, and I have caught trout on it that could not have swallowed it on a bet, they were so small. But I have also caught redfish and trout all day long in bright sun with them, which drew attention at the dock. To me there is nothing more exciting in fishing than to be "walking the dog" with a big Super Spook and have a twenty-inch-plus trout smash it. One thing it took me a long time to learn is not to set the hook until I felt the line come tight. A knee-jerk reaction usually results in a missed fish. Often trout will swipe at the bait or slap it, but miss it. How they miss all those treble hooks is beyond me. I can get them hung up in midair. When this happens, I let the bait lie still on the surface for a few moments. Many times they will hit it again while it is lying stationary. If not, I start walking it again and get ready. Another little trick that works well, if in fact you have a strike and miss it, is to have a rod rigged with a soft plastic and pitch it in the strike zone. That fish is very likely still there, and often it will eat the soft plastic. Redfish on the flats are really a hoot to catch with topwater baits. Often you will see them pushing a wake behind the bait as they catch up with it, and as their mouths are underslung, they almost have to come out of the water partway to pounce on the bait from above. It's not unusual for them to make three or four attempts at catching it before they finally get a hook in their mouths. Those are several exciting moments for the angler, believe me.

Quincy's redfish

Chapter 20

Tackle

The majority of my fishing is done inshore, with most of the fish caught weighing ten pounds or less. My goal for my clients is to make fishing as much fun as possible. I use lightweight tackle. There are a large number of manufacturers making tackle that suits our needs, and personal preference is the final factor in choosing rods. I fish with seven-foot graphite spinning rods. I find that a medium light with a fast action suits my needs for most of the type of fishing I do inshore. I recently switched all my rods out to a Redbone. They are plenty light for the client to get a good fight out of a fish, yet also have enough backbone in them to handle a bigger fish if necessary. Full cork handles with Fuji alloy guides and graphite rod seats ensure I will get plenty of use out of them. I like to match them with 2500- or 3000-class spinning reels. I am currently fishing Shimano Stradic reels and am also in the process of trying out a few Quantum Smokes. My reels catch the devil from hard use, and I go through quite a few. I have found that it does pay to buy higher-end reels, as they tend to stand up better in the long run, thus being worth the extra bucks up front. Have them cleaned regularly, and you should get a lot of years out of them if you are just a weekend fisherman. As for line, I have been using PowerPro braided line for a number of years. Braid works really well in my system of fishing, as it floats, whereas monofilament sinks. I don't have to worry about clients getting their lines nicked down in the shells with the braid. I have settled on twenty-pound test as being the best all-around weight for both casting and holding up to bigger fish. Braid does require a little more care in knot tying, but it works fine with the knots I use—the fisherman's knot, the MirrOLure loop knot, and the surgeon's knot—for connecting the braid to a monofilament leader. My hook selection has narrowed down considerably through the years. Owner Mutu Light Wire circle hooks fill the bill for me day in and day out. They work fine with either cut bait or dead shrimp and are the ticket for live bait. They allow a shrimp to have good movement in the water, as they are a very light wire, and this helps with the bite. I use a size 1/0 hook most of the time, but I may drop down to a size 1 for trout. Hard hooksets are not required, as a fish will almost hook itself every time with the right drag setting. Simply pick up on the rod and go to reeling when the line comes tight. Nine times out of ten, the fish will be hooked in the corner of its mouth, and we kill fewer fish by gut hooking them than we would with a standard J hook. I like to release live fish.

The last thing I want to mention is drag settings. For some reason, a number of people like to have their drags tightened to the point that a freight train couldn't pull line off their reels. I'm sure that can help move fish off the oyster shells or out of the grass, but there is a major disadvantage to it also. That is when the fish is close to the boat. Ninety percent of all fish I see lost are at the boat. Drag is a big part of the culprit. With not very much line out, a fish that makes that final lunge to get away will often pull the hook out of its mouth, simply because the reel won't give out any line to ease the force of the sudden pull. A drag setting that allows a bigger fish to pull line when he is making those hard runs is what I try to achieve. Big trout are notorious for coming off at the boat, and that is exactly the reason: they have soft mouths to begin with and make those big runs at the end of the fight. Loosen up your drags. Have fun catching that fish, and catch more of them.

Boatside tarpon

Conclusion

I hope perhaps that in reading of my adventures, you have found a little bit of humor or a tidbit here or there that has brightened your day and perhaps made a positive impact on your life. I have so enjoyed the opportunity I have had to meet so many wonderful people in my fishing business. In today's world, it seems to me that folks spend a lot more time on electronics and computers and iPads than they should and are missing out on so many pleasures that God gave us to enjoy while on this earth. I especially think kids are the real victims. Looking back on my childhood, I am so thankful for all the time I spent in the great outdoors and for the many memories it provided. Kids today are certainly influenced by social media and the easy access they have to any topic they choose—not all of them good. I'm sure that electronics have their place in our world, but if you want to change a kid's life forever, take him fishing. Certainly not all will take to the sport, but I will bet my last dollar a number of them will, and it will be a life-changing event for them. They will become engrossed in something that is a positive influence and that they can do well into old age. I spent last Saturday with a friend and his dad fishing in the surf off one of our barrier islands. We caught a number of fish, but that is not the picture that is ingrained in my mind about that trip. It is of this ninety-year-old dad standing in the surf next to me, fishing rod in hand bent double as a black drum tried to wrestle itself free from the man who was enjoying the fight almost as much as he likely did when he was six years old. It just never gets old. God bless you and yours, and tight lines to all.

CPSIA information can be obtained
at www.ICGtesting.com
Printed in the USA
BVOW11s2151120118
505186BV00002B/2/P